ISBN: 1-5[illegible]

I Remember Reggie White

Reggie White's premature death in December 2004 shocked the sports world. How could this phenomenal fortress of muscle and mind exit so young at age forty-three? Those who observed him from a distance will remember the pinnacle moment of White's professional football career: a championship ball-capped, T-shirted White jogging around the perimeter of the Louisiana Superdome and holding high the trophy he and the Green Bay Packers had just earned in Super Bowl XXXI.

While many NFL greats leave an indelible stamp on the field, not as many make their mark as exemplary human beings. Those closest to Reggie clearly saw that distinction. *I Remember Reggie White* presents the recollections and favorite stories of this dynamic minister and pro football's Minister of Defense as captured through interviews with teammates, friends, coaches, acquaintances, and members of the media. The narrative spans White's career from his days at Chattanooga (Tenn.) Howard High School, the University of Tennessee, and the now-defunct USFL Memphis Showboats through his NFL career with the Philadelphia Eagles and the Green Bay Packers.

Reggie White left behind a massive legacy. A thirteen-time Pro Bowler and consensus two-time Defensive Player of the Year, he retired as the NFL's all-time

CONTINUED ON BACK FLAP

CONTINUED FROM FRONT FLAP

sack leader. Selected to the NFL's Seventy-fifth Anniversary All-Time Team in 1994, he still holds the Super Bowl single-game sack record.

While football became his burning ambition at a young age, an equally passionate devotion to God and a genuine dedication to ministering led to Reggie's ordination as a Baptist minister at age seventeen. Often controversial for his observations on race and religion, he spent much of his time after retirement from pro football following the 2000 season studying Hebrew and translating the Old Testament text.

ALAN ROSS is a freelance writer and former editor for *American Profile* magazine, Professional Team Publications, and Athlon Sports Communications. A regular contributor to *Lindy's Pro Football* annual, the Sporting News Special Collectors Editions, and the Arizona Cardinals and San Diego Chargers media/fan publications, he has written fifteen books, including *The Yankees Century, The Red Sox Century, Packer Pride, Cubs Pride, Cardinals Glory,* and *Browns Glory.* He lives with his wife, Caroline, in Bisbee, Arizona.

JACKET DESIGN: GORE STUDIO, INC.
JACKET PHOTOGRAPH: AP/WIDE WORLD

CUMBERLAND HOUSE
PUBLISHING INC.

I Remember
Reggie White

I Remember REGGIE WHITE

Friends, Teammates, and Coaches Talk about the NFL's "Minister of Defense"

Alan Ross

Cumberland House
Nashville, Tennessee

Published by
Cumberland House Publishing, Inc.
431 Harding Industrial Drive
Nashville, TN 37211–3160

Cover design: Gore Studio, Inc.
Text design: John Mitchell
Research/administrative assistant: Ariel Robinson

Special thanks to Mrs. Helen Bowman, daughter of former Philadelphia Eagles defensive line coach Dale Haupt, for photo contributions from her family's private library. Acknowledgment as well to Jim Biever for the use of his photos.

Library of Congress Cataloging-in-Publication Data

Ross, Alan, 1944-
I remember Reggie White : friends, teammates, and coaches talk about the nfl's "Minister of Defense" / Alan Ross.
p. cm.
Includes bibliographical references and index.
1. White, Reggie—Friends and associates. 2. Football players—United States—Biography. I. Title.
GV939.W43R67 2005
796.332'092—dc22

2005016068

ISBN 978-1-68442-174-9 (hc)
ISBN 978-1-68442-173-2 (pbk)

For Sara, Jeremy, Jecolia, and Thelma White,
may this one day become an item treasured for its
valued recollections of husband, father, son

and for Caroline,
thank you, my heart, for your constant,
loyal, and deeply devoted love

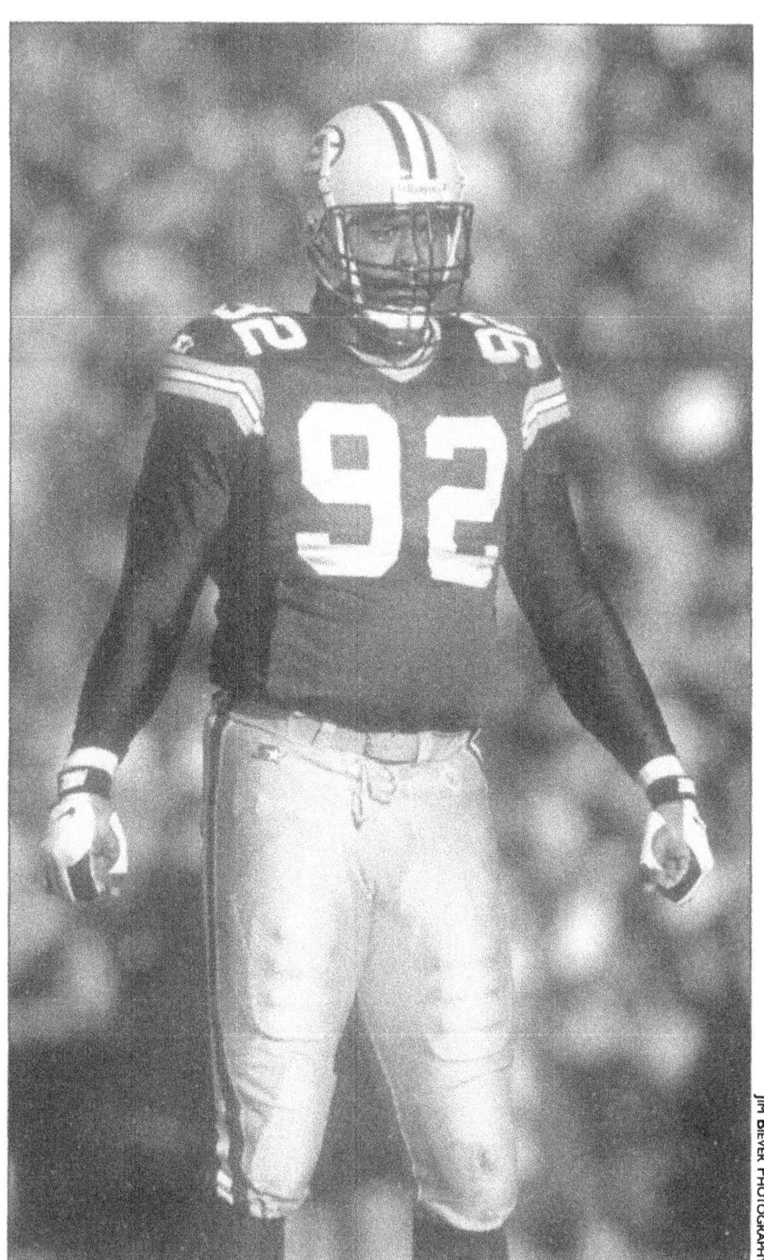

Jim Biever Photography

Contents

FOREWORD

I used to think that Billy Joel's "Only the Good Die Young" was a presumptuous theme, an attempt at tugging a tad too mightily on the melodramatic, especially when the hit song dealt only with teen angst and sidestepped the issue of death completely. Yet it was hard to ignore those lost young icons, particularly in music, who seemed to disappear every thirty seconds during the tempestuous sixties and seventies. That was real, but not entirely unexpected, considering the lifestyle back then.

But the death at age forty-three of professional football giant Reggie White, on December 26, 2004, seemed altogether unreal and even preposterous, like snow in July in Miami. The earth, in an unnatural action, had tilted on its axis. The good, indeed, had died young.

Like so many who viewed Reggie White from a distance, I knew most of the basics of his phenomenal gridiron career and a little bit of the outspoken, impassioned, off-field endeavors that had occasionally enveloped White throughout his years.

I knew he lived with a deeply religious perspective on life, and that it had been engrained in him early.

Never in my dreams did I imagine that I would one day get an opportunity to become acquainted with the awe-inspiring magnitude of this athlete/family man/minister/comic/businessman/motivator/human rights champion/seeker through the intimate, honest, respectful, humorous, forthright, and loving remembrances of Reggie's friends, teammates, coaches, media members, opponents, partners, fans, and associates. Out of a sincere regard for the loss suffered by Mrs. Sara Copeland White, Reggie's widow; their two children, Jeremy and Jecolia; and Reggie's mother, Thelma, no attempt was made to contact family members for interviews. In a statement to the media on the day her husband died, Sara White had expressed to everyone that "we want to thank you in advance for honoring our privacy." I took no small pride in upholding that request.

With deepest gratitude I thank the following for voluntarily contributing their time and recollections of their friend and fallen brother in interviews for this book:

Henry Bowles, Mark Burwell, Calvin Clark, Chuck Dickerson, Santana Dotson, Phillip Fulmer, Willie Gault, Mike Golic, Dale Haupt, Lee Jenkins, Sean Jones, Johnny Majors, Larry Marmie, Raleigh McKenzie, Hardy Nickerson, Herman Prater Sr., Robert Pulliam, Mike Quick, Pepper Rodgers, Clyde Simmons, and Tony Walter.

A special note of thanks to my assistant Ariel Robinson for her tireless work in transcription and research, and the people of Cumberland House, most notably Ron Pitkin and my editor, John Mitchell, for their encouragement and support throughout.

Reggie, we barely knew ye. But I've loved the time spent with you these past months. And while it isn't very likely that the Ithacan king Odysseus was thinking of you when he was smiting the Trojans with his terrible swift sword, I can't help but think of a certain force within professional football who once wreaked havoc on opposing offenses with the fury that could well have inspired these words:

If they ever tell my story,
Let them say I walked with giants
— Odysseus

— A. R.

I Remember
REGGIE WHITE

1

When You Hear the Words "Reggie White"

In assembling ideas for this book, I had wondered what some of the people personally interviewed, the ones who knew Reggie White best, would say about this unique man when asked what first came to mind when they heard the words *Reggie White*. Here's what they said:

Calvin Clark, *teammate and defensive end, United States Football League's Memphis Showboats (1984–85):*

I always called him "the big kid." He just had an innocence about him. When he was around you, he added life to you. Just the talent that he had! He could always entertain a crowd. He brought a great spirit of life to whosever presence he was in.

Chuck Dickerson, *White's defensive line coach with the USFL's Memphis Showboats (1984–85):*

I think you have to think about a dominant personality: a guy that walks into a room and fills it up with his aura. A man that just generates a feeling of . . . "come to me, be around me." He had a magnetism about him that was just special.

Santana Dotson, *three-year teammate at Green Bay and overall ten-year defensive tackle with the Tampa Bay Buccaneers, Green Bay Packers, and Washington Redskins:*

You think of his iconic personality. It's not even his personality, just the man himself—the larger-than-life figure. In his first year in the league, I was a freshman or sophomore in high school. You look at all the ruckus and noise that he's making in the NFL, and when you hear the name Reggie White, an almost larger-than-life picture comes to mind.

Phillip Fulmer, *head coach at the University of Tennessee and offensive line coach during White's years with the Volunteers:*

There are so many. Reggie was the best football player in his senior year that I have seen in college football. That includes some awful good ones that have been through here, and some good ones that we have seen and played against. His senior year, I have never seen anybody dominate games like he did.

Willie Gault, *White's roommate and three-year teammate at UT; NFL opponent with the Chicago Bears and Oakland Raiders:*

A giant. And just a heckuva person, a great person.

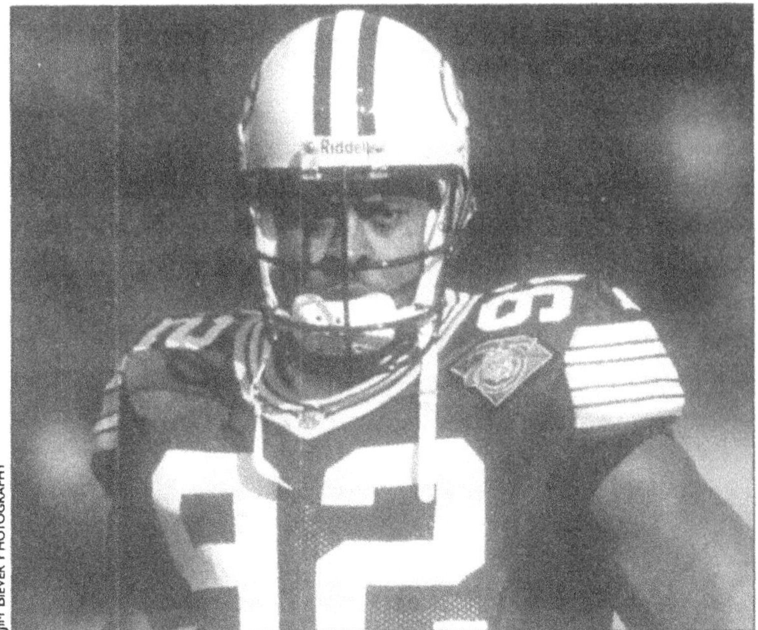

Jim Biever Photography

Reggie White: Consummate player, minister, humorist, friend.

Mike Golic, *White's six-year teammate and fellow defensive linemate with the Philadelphia Eagles:*

The first thing that comes to mind is a once-in-a-lifetime athlete. Because that's the way I first *saw* him. Obviously, after befriending him and being a teammate of his for six years, that changed to what a great man he was, forgetting the football side of it, the sports side of it. He was such a good guy. He believed very much in his convictions. He didn't ram them down your throat, but he was very strong in his convictions.

Dale Haupt, *Philadelphia defensive line coach during White's years with the Eagles:*

He was a great guy to coach. Very productive. Golly, he had so many pass-rush techniques. If one didn't work, he would counter with the other one. He was just unbelievable to stop. You couldn't stop him. Offensive linemen, boy, they were shaking in their boots on Sunday morning. What a great job he did. He didn't like to do Up-Downs, though, [laughing] the old grass drill.

Lee Jenkins, *two-year starting cornerback during White's four seasons at Tennessee:*

Conviction, meaning that he believed strongly in what he believed. Another word would be *friend*. *Friend* and *conviction*.

Sean Jones, *three-year teammate and thirteen-year defensive end with the Los Angeles Raiders, Houston Oilers, and Green Bay Packers:*

The first word that comes to mind would be *complex*. Different dynamics come into play. He was a fun-loving guy: "Okay let's joke, but let's not joke about this, 'cause I don't play around with this [God and religion]." He could've just made a your-mama's-so-fat joke, but then it might be, "I understand, but we're talking about God right now, so I don't joke about that."

Johnny Majors, *head coach, University of Tennessee (1977–92):*

The most dominating defensive player that I have seen in college football, that I have coached in football, over a four-year period.

~

Larry Marmie, *University of Tennessee defensive coordinator in White's senior season:*

Personality. I thought Reggie was a very engaging and fun person. He was very aware, had a great sense of humor, and was a guy who enjoyed a good practical joke. He could laugh at himself; a guy who really enjoyed people. The more you think about it, the more things come to your mind. He was just a person who enjoyed people and was very fun-loving and sincere in his relationships.

~

Raleigh McKenzie, *three-year teammate at Tennessee; sixteen-year NFL veteran and frequent NFL opponent with the Washington Redskins:*

Good friend.

~

Hardy Nickerson, *friend and sixteen-year linebacker with Pittsburgh, Tampa Bay, Jacksonville, and Green Bay:*

Respect, man of God, great husband, great father. The thing that jumps out at me is just his sincerity and loyalty as a friend. Lastly, the greatest defensive lineman that ever lived.

~

Mike Quick, *wide receiver, Philadelphia Eagles (1982–90); six-year teammate of White:*

I smile. Because that's kind of what the brother did for me. A *very* special person. The nice thing about it, if he were still right here, I would say the same thing that I'm saying now.

~

Pepper Rodgers*, head coach of the Memphis Showboats (1983–85):*

First thing that comes to mind is that he was a terrific guy. He was a fun fellow; he had a great sense of humor, and he just had a heart of gold. You could say, "Yeah, but what about Reggie, the player?" Well, there are a lot of great players out there that don't have all that stuff that I just said about Reggie.

~

Clyde Simmons*, fellow defensive lineman for seven of White's eight years in Philadelphia:*

Friend. There are a lot of things that come up when you speak of him: the jokes played on him, played by him."

~

Tony Walter*, assistant metro editor, Green Bay Press-Gazette:*

The first thing that comes to mind is the leadership, the spiritual leadership. Reggie kind of entered into a different category from everybody else. It was combined with his immense talent, which automatically elevated him in a lot of people's eyes. He used that talent to affect other people, not only with his leadership on the football team, but with his faith, with his humanity. He was just an impact player, an impact person; just a unique individual in so many different ways.

2

Early Reggie

In 1961, Chattanooga, Tennessee, long known as the home of the historic Chattanooga Choo-Choo, was the site of a most uncommon birthing: a six-pound boy who would weigh more than thirty pounds just three months later, a child who eschewed baby food for table food. At seven, he looked more like he was thirteen; a man-child and future NFL star, who concurrently developed into an impassioned disciple of God. Two disparate personal destinations uniquely housed within the same human being.

Reggie White grew up in the Painted Wood section of south Chattanooga. At age seven, he was offered a choice that ultimately would affect the rest of his life: he could join his mother and her second husband, Leonard Collier, serving out his one remaining year of a service hitch at Fort Riley in Manhattan, Kansas, or he could stay put in his hometown under the supervision of his grandmother, Mildred Dodds. The youngster chose Chattanooga. Through the influence of his caring grandmother, White was brought face to face with his

God, embarking on a lifelong devotion that would eventually touch thousands of people, creating heartache and mental anguish for White, as well as a pervasive happiness and sense of well being.

White's early walk indicated he was on an accelerated spiritual path. Saved at age thirteen, he became an ordained Baptist minister by seventeen, unashamedly and confidently taking that ministry out into his world at Chattanooga Howard High School, where he developed into an all-state football and basketball player.

Side by side with White on that journey, upon her return to Chattanooga, was his mother Thelma, who taught her son how to stand up for himself and what he believed in, and most importantly, to relentlessly pursue his dreams.

"She made me feel special and taught me to believe that I am just as important as any other person—no more, no less," said White in his autobiography, *In the Trenches*. "She had a very strong work ethic, and she was diligent to pass that work ethic on to her children. . . . She demanded our respect—but what's more, she earned it, along with our love and admiration. . . . Throughout my high school and college sports careers, she came to all my games, and so did my two aunts. . . . My mother, Thelma Collier, has always been one of my heroes."[1]

White's interest in football was kick-started around the age of twelve, when he first saw O. J. Simpson tear up and down a football field for the Buffalo Bills. As kids everywhere express a desire to emulate their heroes, White became inspired viewing Simpson. But instead of wishing to lug the pigskin, White wanted to be the one to smash head-on into the Hall of Fame runner and nail him in his tracks.

As White was eventually bound for a basketball career as well at Howard High School, it was only natural that a few hardwood heroes entered the picture, too. Filling that role were two accomplished pros with the then-American Basketball Association: Julius Erving—the great Dr. J—and former North Carolina star Bobby Jones. The latter, whom White met at a sports camp, later became a Christian role model for White as well.

Even before he entered high school, the buzz about the young Chattanooga athlete began circulating throughout the area. Henry W. Bowles, who coached White in both basketball and also as a position coach in football at Howard, remembers his first impressions of White as a youngster.

"I first met Reggie when he was about nine years old," says Bowles. "I was doing some recreation work during the summer months, running a portable recreation wagon. I would go through his neighborhood about once a week. When I first saw him, the kids were playing what they called 'Four Square.' As I was observing the kids, I noticed he wasn't doing too well; he never got out of the first square. His coordination and reflexes just weren't there. I made a statement regarding that to the playground director at the time, who I didn't know was his cousin.

"'Look at that young man,' I said. 'He doesn't seem to be reacting too well. Something wrong with him?'

"'Mr. Bowles, that's my cousin,' she said. She got attitude with it. 'Ain't nothin' wrong with him. He's only nine. Those other boys are twelve, thirteen, fourteen, fifteen years old!'

"Reggie was as big as them," continues Bowles. "He had the height. I didn't know how young he was, so I told her, 'Look here, we're going to develop a program for the younger kids.' And I worked out a physical fitness program for her, for the whole group by age groups. They would do a lot of running and develop the big muscles.

"'You work on these things on Mondays and Fridays,' I told her, 'and I'll do it on Wednesdays when I come. You gotta have a program for them before they eat their lunch to let 'em know that, if they're gonna eat lunch here, they gotta do these things.'

"I talked with the principal at the school, who asked if I would design a playground for them, with a softball field," says Bowles, who retired from Howard in 1998 after serving a total of thirty-nine years at the high school. "They didn't have anything like that in this area at the time. I did that for the principal, and she got it done. The next year, we got all these activities going."

As it turned out, young Reggie wasn't the first relative in the White clan to come to Bowles's attention. Bowles had played baseball for White's grandfather, Clarence Dodd, and even coached White's father, Charles White, also a graduate of Howard.

"At the time his daddy came through, I was the backfield coach and offensive coordinator," remembers Bowles. "His daddy was on the team for one or two years when I first started coaching. Later on, we played together on Reggie's grandfather's team."

So, football was in the family, too. But before football, White's favorite sport, early on, had been baseball.

"Apparently he was pretty good at it at a young age," says Bowles. "But when I mentioned baseball to him, when I first met him, and told him that I had played ball with his daddy and his granddaddy, he never mentioned that baseball was his favorite sport. I just wanted him to know that I knew the family."

Bowles doesn't deny that there were ulterior motives behind his conversation with the promising prospect.

"At that time, McCallie and some of the other private schools were trying to get Reggie," recalls Bowles. "I was just trying to lay the framework by letting him know that I knew his family very well, to influence him in coming our direction. I said, 'Where you thinking about going to school?'

"'Don't worry,' he said. 'I'm going to Howard.' That's all I wanted to hear."

The young sports prodigy had the school coaches drooling with possibilities. Bowles had the opportunity to work with White at a position that some observers might find interesting in light of the future NFLer's success on defense but that nonetheless points to White's superior athleticism.

"I was not the head football coach at Howard," Bowles says, "but Reggie was in my specialty group. I was coaching the wide receivers and tight ends at the time, and he was in my position group. He played tight end and he played defense everywhere: nose tackle, left tackle, wherever we needed him, and wherever the other team was strongest, that's where he played.

"The first day he reported—it was on a Monday—I had gone and heard John Stallworth, the Pittsburgh Steelers' outstanding wide receiver, give a speech. I told Reggie about meeting Stallworth and said, 'You know, as a young man, your *thigh* is bigger than his whole body.' That's what I told Reggie. 'You've got a million-dollar body,' I said. 'If you work hard enough, it'll pay off for you.'

"I don't know whether that stuck with him or not, but he was a hard worker and had a great work ethic. He was the type of guy that, no matter how much you put on him, he never complained. He always came back with, 'What's next, Coach, what's next?' while the rest of the players would be complaining. I thought that was something very special about him. He was just a go-getter, a hard worker."

White's head football coach at Howard, Robert Pulliam, a three-year starter at left defensive tackle at the University of Tennessee, from 1972 through 1974, remembers his first impression of the youth he would one day mentor at Howard.

"The first time I met him, I will never forget it," says Pulliam. "I had a chance to visit with him at the junior high school where he was at. I had a chance to visit with him one-on-one, and I began by asking him about his goals, what he wanted to do with his life. I hadn't been too long finished playing at the University of Tennessee. Most school age kids had seen me play. So, initially I thought the guy was going to tell me he wanted to be a great defensive lineman, and of course, I had already practiced a great answer for it: 'Hey, I'm your man. I'm a great defensive lineman! And I could teach you how to do that.'

"But instead of telling me that, the first thing he uttered to me was that he wanted to be a minister. At that point, being a very, very young football coach, it kind of knocked me on my heels. In the end, we went forth and started cultivating a relationship to have him enter our high school."

While Pulliam looked forward to the day when his young prospect would first suit up in a Tigers uniform, he wasn't prepared for a noticeable flaw that accompanied White on the field, one that would rigorously define a somewhat adversarial (though intentional on Pulliam's part) relationship between coach and player.

"Very quickly I found out the strength, the size—all the potential was there," recollects Pulliam, upon seeing White firsthand. "But he had a tremendously kind spirit about him. I remember, even in high school, his first year playing for me, that Reggie was one of the most coachable people I've ever had the privilege of working with. One of those things where you would ask him to do anything—run through a brick wall—he would, no hesitation. He would die trying.

"As a young player, a high school sophomore, if I were to call time out and tell Reggie to hit the player he was up against in the mouth, he would hit him in the mouth. But on his own, he just wanted to be kind and play with people. That was the first thing that I wanted to try to instill in him: to up his level of aggressiveness but still keep it within the confines of the sport."

Pulliam continues: "First of all, football is a game. You're matching wits against the person opposite you, and within those seconds that you run a play, you want to engage and compete as best you can to defeat the individual in front of you. When you look at a lot of players, they have that fire up under 'em. They line up in their stance and are prepared to unleash major physical aggression towards the person opposite them.

"So, I had to find a way to prepare Reggie for beating that. You can't sit there with a smile on your face when that guy's got a frown. You sit there too long with that smile, he's going to get the best of you."

What Pulliam carried out to impress that fact on young Reggie has become legend at Howard and initially created a schism between the two, with White believing he was being unfairly set upon, while his mentor was convinced a man was being molded in his midst. Coach Bowles was an interested observer of the developing interplay between the two.

"Robert did a lot to inspire Reggie," recalls Bowles. "He would challenge Reggie a lot of times in the weight room. After the football season was over, they'd have a little one-on-one basketball. I played Robert. I was an old man, and he was a young man about twenty-two years of age just coming out of college. He still had that serious competitive spirit. Man, he would lay it on me, but I could take it pretty good at that time.

"But he and Reggie were in there one day playing ball so rough that I had to stay out there and referee. I was afraid to leave the gym. Robert was trying to bring that mean streak out of Reggie, and Reggie would not back up from it. It got so bad, blood started showing up here and there. I had to take the ball, lock it up, and wouldn't let them have it. Then sometimes Robert would take Reggie to the weight room, into the wrestling room, and they would scuffle around down there on the mat."

Pulliam continued the schooling of his star pupil relentlessly, pushing it right to the limit.

"From the first moment I met him, I knew this kid had a big future," says Pulliam. "But as a young coach, over the years looking back, my God, what in the world was I thinking? How could such a young coach believe he could see so much potential in a person at that very young age? And I was very young myself. Basically, I felt that, with the confession he gave me [about wanting to become a minister], I had an obligation to do what I had to do to make some of those beliefs come true. From day one, I forecast most of the things that happened with Reggie.

"Prior to the legendary basketball games, before he enrolled at the school, I had him over to my apartment," adds Pulliam. "At one point, I went inside to fix hamburgers and check on everything. While I was gone, he was out there playing. He was in a pickup game with some guys that I used to play with who were around my age. When I came back I noticed that there was no smile on Reggie's face, he was kind of down.

"I watched for a little bit, talked to some people, and come to find out these guys roughed him up a little bit. Being a young boy, he didn't know quite how to handle that. So I saw that as a perfect opportunity for me to seize and captivate his heart. Big brother, you know. I immediately entered the game and set about thrashing those guys that had tried to rough Reggie up and intimidate him. From that point on, there was no doubt of the closeness of the friendship and the bond that Reggie and I had, because I kind of stepped to the plate and took up for him.

"But my playing days were over. I couldn't go back out on the field and take his uniform and whip people for him. We headed into the winter basketball season, and I decided that, as much as I cared about him, I had to show tough love and actually take a risk on shattering our friendship."

Pulliam recounts how his role as mentor and big brother came with a big price, but one that the young coach was determined to deliver for the betterment of his "younger brother."

"I didn't have any brothers," says Pulliam, "but you watch TV, you read the books, and you talk about that older brother. It was the kind of situation where the older brother, at times, doesn't look like he really cares about that younger brother. It matters in times when the older brother might reach an age and go off to college or go off to the military, and that younger brother is left to fend for himself in the neighborhood. That older brother knows some of the pitfalls, the bullying, and whatnot, and he will take measures into his own hands and actually administer some minor thrashing to prepare that young brother. And so it was with those basketball games.

"I remember fondly Coach Bowles overseeing one in particular," Pulliam recalls. "Ol' Reggie's sitting there, and I had gotten him to the point of crying. Coach Bowles called for a little intermission, so I went out and got a drink of water and sucked some oxygen. Coach Bowles handily ushered everyone else back into the gym, and then he came up to me.

"'Now Coach, we just got him,' he said. 'It's his first year here, and there are schools all around the area that would love for this young man to get upset and transfer. Looking at the relationship that you guys have, Coach. You can't let him go home feeling the way he feels, or we might lose him.'

"I listened to Coach Bowles, but when he got everybody away, he sent Reggie outside to the steps to visit with me so I could console him. I took one look and saw those tears streaming down. He was really hurt because that big brother had just thrashed him and he was almost wondering, 'To thrash me like that, do you still care about me?' Something told me at that point that this was the defining moment. But I couldn't let my heart speak and say, 'Okay, look here, I'm sorry' and try to explain it to him. Instead, I looked at him.

"'Reggie, now if you think I called you out here to apologize to you, you might as well get your big butt back in there in the paint, and I'll be in to finish you off in a moment.' I said, 'What I want to do is prepare you. I am going to tell you that, until you get to a point where you are confident enough within yourself to stand toe-to-toe matching me, I'm going to thrash you every chance I get.'

"And I promised him that I was going to continue to roughhouse him till we got to that point. To be honest with you—and I don't think I've ever told anyone this—it didn't last long, about two weeks."

What followed at the end of that fortnight was a life-changing moment for White, as far as Pulliam is concerned. A charity basketball game at Howard pitted the student-athletes against the faculty. Now on display before the entire school would be another much-talked-about White vs. Pulliam matchup on the court.

"The school, the community, everybody in Chattanooga knew about that big basketball game!" recalls Pulliam. "It was a fund-raiser, a lot of fun around the school, but you don't expect to have people hanging from the rafters for it. As we were warming up getting ready for the game, it was like, my gracious, I'm seeing every teacher, every student I'm teaching, I'm seeing people all over! That gym was filled like a dadgum championship playoff game.

"Not being real smart, initially I wasn't real sure why these people would throw so much support to this event. Then, right before tip-off, I start looking around, and I'm like, 'Wait a minute, gettin' a little warm to me now. These people might be coming here to accost me because of that previous game [with Reggie]!'

"But as we began, right within the first four minutes, Reggie and I got into a close-vest situation. I went up for a rebound, had the ball, and started to come down with it over my head. Suddenly I realized that the ball wasn't coming down with me. It was staying up there. Next thing I knew, I was being pulled over Reggie's shoulder and landed flat on the floor. You could have heard a pin drop in the gym. Nobody knew what to expect. I remembered looking at Reggie's face, and he had that look like, 'Man, I ain't reaching no hand down to lift you up. I'm not apologizing. Are you ready for more?'

"At that point I knew Reggie was now someone who could take that same aggressiveness out onto the field. People were waiting to see what I would do. I just got up, moved past him, and ran down to the other end of the court, because the lesson had been learned. It was really a proud moment in a way, seeing that exact instant when Reggie came of age."

White achieved All-State status in football while at Howard, but his athletic expression wasn't limited to the gridiron. He also proved to be a dominant force in basketball, surely due in no small part to the psychological "makeover" supplied by football coach Robert Pulliam in their private—and public—battles on the court.

Henry Bowles, White's basketball coach, wasn't initially sure where his young athlete's interests lay, but remembers giving the youngster a little piece of advice.

"I didn't know if he was that interested in playing basketball at the very beginning," says Bowles, "but I used to tell him all the time, 'You know, all those agility drills in basketball can't help but make you a better football player.' Even then, he was determined to be the best he could be."

With a chuckle, Bowles recalls one courtside story involving White while the Howard team was in Memphis for a Thanksgiving weekend tournament. Sometimes, as White found out, when there's just no place to hide in a gymnasium filled with the opposition's fans, an ability to laugh at yourself is a good thing.

"I would always introduce them to some of the better teams over there in Memphis," Bowles recalls. "Each year, they would either come to Chattanooga or we would go there. This particular season we were over there and were down like thirteen points at halftime, but we had come back and made a tremendous run. For some reason, Reggie didn't get back down the floor. We stole the ball and he was still right down there. We threw the ball to him, but instead of maybe going up with one hand and layin' it in, Reggie was gonna do a two-hand dunk. Well, he hit the ball on the front of the rim and fell flat on his back!

"I walked out on the floor and circled him; I was checking the floor with my feet. Then I went back and took my seat. The people in the stands, they laughed themselves to death. Reggie was so embarrassed; he got up and took off running to the other end of the court just as fast as he could. He couldn't help but start laughing himself."

For the Howard players, an out-of-town trip was a pretty big deal. Boys being boys, matters like curfew rules were just so many small obstacles to circumvent, even when the freedom excursion amounted to nothing more than an innocent act, yet an action that undoubtedly would come with a price.

"That same night—we'd had a big meal—I told the fellows that we were going to bed at twelve o'clock and nobody was to be out of their room after twelve," says Bowles. "Well, Reggie loved to eat, and he hit one of those hungry spells. He wound up skipping out of the room and going downstairs to a vending machine. I did my bed check, and when I went into his room, his bed was not totally full. What he had done, he had put two pillows together in the bed and put the cover over them.

"Charles Morgan was his roommate. They were so big, they had to sleep by themselves. I was pretending I was talking to somebody else outside the room, 'These guys are all in their beds. That's one good thing about my kids, they all obey rules and regulations around here.' Then I slipped into the bathroom of Reggie and Charles's room and closed the door, with the lights off. About three minutes later, Reggie knocked on the door. Morgan jumped up out of the bed.

"'Coach been here, man,' said Morgan, 'but he didn't know you were gone.'

"When he said that, I jumped out of the bathroom and cut the light on," Bowles says, laughing. "Scared him to death! So the next night, Reggie did not dress; he didn't play. You hate it when somebody breaks a rule, but you've also got to establish that whatever you say is what you mean. On the way back to Chattanooga, we stopped and ate. I brought two or three pieces of chicken back, 'cause I didn't eat 'em all, and I offered him the chicken. Reggie took it and ate it, then said, 'Coach, I believe you're trying to bribe me.' I said, 'You've got the picture wrong. *You're* the one in trouble. You oughta be bribing *me*!'"

White didn't let the matter end there, though. Feeling the suspension in Memphis had been a bit unfair, he enlisted the help of a relative to speak on his behalf to Bowles.

"He had his granddaddy come over and talk with me," says Bowles. "His granddaddy had probably done some of this same stuff back when we played for him. He said, 'Coach, I don't want you to get upset because I'm comin'. Reggie wanted me to come, and I'm here. Whatever you decide, I'm going to go along with it, because I know you're going to be fair.'

"'Look here,' I told him, 'I just had to teach him a lesson. This is the beginning of the season, and the team knows that if I'd do this to Reggie, I'll do it to them. Reggie's got to understand that he's not above the law.'

"It worked out," says Bowles. "He missed the next ball game, the opening ball game of the season. I told his granddaddy to have Reggie come see me. I said, 'You don't have to tell 'im *I* said it, but what he needs to do is come back here and apologize.' We let him back after those consequences, of course, and that was just great because I never had any trouble with anyone else the whole year.

"Sometimes, it's rough to teach a lesson; sometimes the whole group suffers. But in the end, they knew they had to obey and do the things that they should do to be a part of [the team]."

Bowles nearly didn't get the chance to coach White as well as a slew of other Howard basketball players.

"I was asked to take the program for one year, because I was tabbed to become the football coach the year after that," he remembers. "I had coached the junior high program before I went up to the high school. The kids begged and pleaded with me, asking if I would stay with them. They promised that they would carry me to the state tournament for the next two years. Believe it or not, they did. So, I stayed with basketball. One year turned into twenty-nine."

Raleigh McKenzie, who played three years with White at Tennessee and who went on to a sixteen-year NFL career with the Washington Redskins, Philadelphia Eagles, San Diego

Chargers, and Green Bay Packers, remembers meeting White one summer when both were still in their pre-teens.

"We were probably eleven or twelve," says McKenzie of their initial encounter. "He and some friends of his knew my cousin, 'cause all of my family was in Chattanooga for the summer. We played a little neighborhood football, way back when, passing the ball around and just playing a little field football. At that time, Reggie didn't say nothing. We were kind of the same way, too—we didn't talk much.

"He's the one that brought that up [when they reconnected at Tennessee]. He was like [impersonating Reggie's voice in a husky whisper]: 'Hey, I remember you.' And I was like, 'Yeah,' because he said some of the names we knew, and it was like, 'Awww, yeah, I remember that!'"

McKenzie would later attend Knoxville high school powerhouse Austin-East, while White settled in at Howard. He recalls from experience that White wasn't a player you wanted to incite on the field.

"We actually played against each other in high school," says McKenzie, who just missed being teammates with White at both Philadelphia and Green Bay in the NFL. "He was in Chattanooga; we were in Knoxville. We always played a couple of Chattanooga teams, and Reggie was a pretty good player back then, too. He was a tight end and a defensive tackle.

"In a game against us, he was going out for a pass and his quarterback overthrew him, and our safety caught it. I don't think our guy took but about five steps. Reggie got so mad that he didn't get to catch the ball that he tackled our guy and separated [the safety's] shoulder. Ohhh, from that point on, I'm thinking, *Uh- oh. This guy, you don't want to make him mad*. But that was just an example of his good play."

Robert Pulliam remembers the caravan of college recruiters that came calling during White's senior year. It was a lesson in manipulation, overt posturing, and in certain instances, fashioning untruths in the battle to get the upper hand with the hot prospect.

"When it started looking like Tennessee might gain the upper hand for him," says Pulliam, "I remember Reggie sharing with me that someone had come and told him that maybe he needed to go here or there, actually trying to direct him to a school. That's something that even I wouldn't do. When someone was trying to steer him some place, he had an obligation to let me know.

"These people were telling him, 'You don't want to go to the University of Tennessee. I know he's a great man, but Johnny Majors is not a Christian. You need to go here, because this man is a Christian.' I took one look at Reggie and said, 'There's no telling what people can say. You can't let people make your mind up. You have to seek and find it for yourself.'"

Bowles says recruiters came to Howard from all over not just to catch a glimpse of the athletic White but also to get a glimpse of another, equally talented teammate.

"We had another kid at that same time, Charles Morgan," recalls Bowles. "Both he and Reggie wound up going to the same place. It was amazing, when coaches like Terry Donahue (UCLA) and Oklahoma and all these other places started coming through.

"'We're interested in that White boy,' they'd say.

"I'd say, 'Well, we got another kid , too.'

"'Well, we'll take him, if we can get the White boy.'

"'Well, I hope you don't let the kid hear you say that,' I'd say. 'Both of them are blue-chippers. I'll assure you of one thing: If both of them went to the same school, this Morgan kid would probably make the team before Reggie.'

"'Why would you say that?'

"'Reggie is a great kid, but he doesn't have a mean streak in him yet,' I'd tell them.

"Athletics-wise, Morgan's ability was better than Reggie's," says Bowles. "He had agility, coordination, and all those other good things going for him. Both of them were in my group. Morgan eventually left and went to the backfield to play quarterback. Of course, that broke my heart. I'd have much rather seen him playing fullback. I couldn't make that decision, but I did make the recommendation.

"But I also told Morgan, 'If you don't learn to control your attitude, that might hold you back.' The press had told him he was the greatest thing happening. He had trouble after that and wound up leaving the school [UT]."

A harbinger of White's magnetic appeal became evident early on. Robert Pulliam remembers once hearing a fascinating report about the Howard senior's instinctive leadership tendencies.

"The summer right before his senior year," says Pulliam, "Reggie was invited to participate in a summer football camp at the University of Tennessee and actually work as a counselor, while he was still at Howard. I remember the coaches telling me how he was like a Pied Piper with the kids. The other counselors basically didn't have to do anything, because the little kids that they were there to monitor were all with Reggie. They would follow him to the dining hall, everywhere. I mean the whole camp! He'd have all those kids just following him all over campus."

Coach Bowles saw the high-school-aged White morph into a man-child during his four years at Chattanooga Howard.

White's desire to bulk up via weight-lifting became an obsession, and Bowles recounts one lifting episode that gives an indication of the student-athlete's compelling exuberance, pride, and determination.

"We bought a weight machine," says Bowles, "and I remember Reggie was determined to push all those weights up before he graduated. That was on the bench press. Well, he did it. He did it his senior year after football season. He came running up to my office:

"'Got something to show you!' he said. 'Got something to show you!'

"'Reggie, I'm busy,' I said. 'I'm trying to get my lessons [for class] together.'

"'C'mon, Coach! I got something to show you!'

"Well, we went down, and he couldn't do it that day," Bowles continues. "He'd already used up all his energy.

"'I just *did* this, Coach. I can do it!' Reggie said.

"But then, two days later, before he got exhausted again, he asked me to come sit with him down there in the weight room a while," says Bowles. "And then he did it. He bench-pressed every one of them. That would have to be about 300 pounds.

"Reggie would be there after we practiced, because he rode home with me a lot of times during the basketball season, and he'd ride home with Coach Pulliam some during football season. I'd be throwing all my practice clothes into the washing machine and getting stuff ready for the next day, and Reggie would go down to the weight room all by himself and be pushing those weights. Of course, I'd get on him: 'We don't allow you to come down here all by yourself.' But he kept on slipping down there. We never had to stand over him [to get him] to do his workout."

Bowles says there was no question about White's intended direction in life when he first entered Howard.

"I would always inquire of a new group of kids coming here, 'What do you plan to do in life, after you've gotten a scholarship through football?'" says Bowles. "I always put that thought in their minds: Work hard enough, and you'll be rewarded—and your reward could be a good scholarship someplace.

"Reggie said he wanted to be a professional football player. I said, 'Well, the only person that can keep you from becoming a tremendous professional football player is yourself. You've got the physical tools. All you've got to do is develop, develop, develop—mentally as well as physically. And you'll make it, buddy, you'll make it.'"

3

KNOXVILLE

Alabama, UCLA, Oklahoma, Ohio State, Michigan, and Miami all reached for the brass ring, but it was the Tennessee Volunteers of Big Orange Country that grabbed the much-sought-after services of the Chattanooga Howard High School phenom. As a senior, in 1979, Reggie White had been selected the best high school two-sport athlete in the United States over another skilled competitor who would carve his own name in the gallery of sports greatness: Patrick Ewing.

When White headed to "The Hill," [named for the rising bank on the north shore of the Tennessee River that overlooks venerable Neyland Stadium], it had been twenty-four years since a Tennessee player had won the coveted SEC Player of the Year Award. Back in 1955 and 1956, a triple-threat Big Orange tailback playing out of the old single wing named Johnny Majors tore up southern gridirons en route to earning consensus All-America recognition and a runner-up finish in the Heisman Trophy voting, along with selection as the SEC Player of the Year. White wanted to become the next

Orange and White player to garner the latter award, listing it as one of his goals when he came to Tennessee. As events would have it, the Vol legend—Majors—would become White's head coach at UT.

But the leap from the prep ranks to the big-time atmosphere of a major college football program is an eye-opener for many young athletes sheltered in the comfort zone of high school stardom and privilege—the Big Man On Campus syndrome.

That changeover for White is best illustrated in a telling comment he made in his autobiography about his first day of practice with the Volunteers in the fall of 1980.

"I absorbed more physical punishment and verbal abuse than in a month of high school football," said White of that initial session. He claims he then called his mother and told her he was quitting. She reminded him of a commitment he had made to himself and to her while still at Howard, relative to his dream of becoming a pro football player: "As long as God blesses me with the ability to play football, I'm going to give it everything I've got and I'm never gonna give up!"[1]

It was a timely reminder, for White would go on to achieve consensus All-America honors at UT, and yes, become the SEC Player of the Year in 1983.

Majors, a powerful authority figure and state icon from his storybook playing days at Tennessee, helped shape the raw, unfocused energy of the talented White. The relationship was reciprocal from White's end. Majors commanded respect. He'd been there before, first as a top-level player and now as a national championship head coach, having taken the University of Pittsburgh Panthers to the national title in 1976 behind the dazzling performances of All-America running back Tony Dorsett. The following year, he accepted an offer to return to his alma mater.

To say that Majors hung the proverbial moon in his home state is an understatement. He was a living, breathing, full-fledged, unabated legend.

"Every football fan in Tennessee wanted to shake his hand, and every teenage boy wanted to play for him," White once recalled. "I was lucky. I *did* play for him."[2]

Majors, naturally, was a fan of White, calling him the finest defensive player he had ever coached. The former Volunteers head man, now special assistant to the chancellor and athletics director at the University of Pittsburgh, expresses deep, heartfelt feelings when White's name arises.

"He was just a big ol' teddy bear," Majors recalls wistfully, "but man, when it came time to play, he was something else. He went to war when the whistle blew one-on-one, three-on-three, seven-on-seven, or eleven-on-eleven. I mean he was so competitive. It was in his heart and soul to just do it, and do it the best that it can be done. He is one of the greatest football players I ever coached, and he was as good as you can be as a defensive lineman.

"His senior year, I referred to him as the Dorsett of defensive linemen. Dorsett was the greatest football player for four years I ever coached. He only missed one game in four years. Reggie and Dorsett were in the same type of class their senior years. Reggie was also a great player for four years, but his senior year he never got hurt. He could play through some injuries. He had a great senior year. And he could make plays on the opposite side of the line of scrimmage, because people couldn't block him."

One particular game in White's landmark '83 season Majors will never forget. The senior defensive lineman displayed a dominance rarely seen on the fields of play at any level.

"LSU came in there, a good football team, and Reggie just disrupted their entire offensive game plan," says Majors. "He dominated the whole side of the line of scrimmage, which he did many times. He was matched up against a great All-America offensive tackle at LSU. I really wouldn't want to mention his name; I wouldn't want to embarrass him. Reggie just dominated him and that whole side of the line of scrimmage. That was probably the most commanding one-man defensive performance that I witnessed in my career."

Former UT teammate Raleigh McKenzie was awed by White's physical mastery in that October 8 game in Knoxville, won by Tennessee, 20–6.

"Reggie was king," remembers McKenzie. "I swear, he just had one of those days. I think that game helped propel Reggie into the NFL, because he took a great tackle and treated him like he was a high school player. He was just all over the place. He had three or four sacks and all kinds of tackles, and just kind of took the game into his own hands on the defensive side. He showed how dominating one guy can be."

Current Vols head coach Phillip Fulmer recounts a specific play from that LSU game that turned the tide in favor of the Big Orange:

"At a crucial point against LSU, they had a big third-down-and-short play," recalls Fulmer. "I don't know how or why they did it, but they ran right at Reggie. He took the offensive guard and stuck him into the backfield, basically tackled the lead back—the fullback—with one arm and wrapped up the tailback for a two-yard loss with the other arm. It still shows up on highlight films around here."

Larry Marmie, the Vols' defensive coordinator who arrived at Tennessee just in time for White's final season, also comments on that momentous game against the Tigers.

"That game stands out in my mind , too," says Marmie, now defensive coordinator for the NFL's St. Louis Rams. "For lack of a better word, it was probably as dominating a performance as I had ever seen by a person playing any position. He basically took that game over. And that's kind of hard for a defensive tackle—Reggie played both the end and tackle, we moved him around. But he did, he took that game over. And I've even talked to some of the guys who coached at LSU back then, and they would always bring up the same thing, so it must have been obvious to everybody what kind of game he played."

Marmie, a favorite of White at UT for his inspirational rather than scolding manner of mentoring, also recalls that the legendary nickname affixed to White during his career—"the Minister of Defense"—originated in Knoxville.

"The best I can remember, they started using that in his senior year," says Marmie. "I could be wrong, but he became so dominating that year, in the way that he played. I didn't remember hearing that term being used prior to that."

Understandably. White had done little before his senior year to distinguish himself in his play. Though a four-year starter, injuries took their toll in his junior year, and the great things predicted for White failed to materialize before the '83 season.

"When you talk to most of the people who were there then, they felt like, until that time in his career, that, really, Reggie had been somewhat of an underachiever," notes Marmie. "This is what everybody told me when I got there, about how good this guy could be but that he never would be for various reasons, etc. I think the timing was right. Reggie was at a point in his career where he was really hungry.

"There was a connection early on between us when I got there. I could feel it. There were certain things in his character and in his makeup that he respected and that he was looking for. While he showed respect for everyone, regardless of what type of person it may be, if someone shared the same thoughts, interests, sincerity, and trust, then all of those things seemed to fall into place at the right time. He had some terrific teammates on that team, and they all created an atmosphere that particular year that was really special. I think it was special for Reggie, and I think that he felt that. The way he played that year was just unbelievable."

~

As Marmie mentioned, the aggressiveness that characterized White's play his senior season was barely in evidence in the defensive tackle/end's earlier years in Knoxville. Majors noted that fact when asked about a comment that the Vols mentor had made concerning White's assertiveness in 1982. Majors had stated: "I think Reggie White could become the finest defensive lineman I've ever coached before he leaves Tennessee. He should become an outstanding player. He just needs to become tougher and more aggressive."[3]

Two years later, in 1984, Majors made the following assessment: "There won't be anyway to estimate what Reggie meant to us. It's inestimable. He provided humor, leadership, morale."[4]

More than twenty years later Majors comments on his earlier quotes:

"I remember that was my thinking," says Majors. "It reminds me of a guy who's much bigger, stronger, and quicker than everybody else his age, but who probably wasn't as aggressive as he could have been, probably afraid he would hurt other people and beat up on them maybe too much. He got hurt some a little more than you might think, or maybe couldn't play through some pain as much as an experienced, mentally tough guy could do, and that was of some concern to me, even though he started as a freshman.

"He had amazing ability," Majors continues. "You could recognize that right away. The first time I saw it was watching high school films when he was at Howard. I also saw him play basketball in person. His agility and dexterity on the basketball court was so obvious, and he was so much bigger than people that you'd see anywhere in those days. He was a man-child, without question.

"I have recruited and coached all over the country, from California to the East Coast and from the Great Lakes down to Florida, but I don't think I've seen anybody who was more impressive physically and had more natural ability than Reggie White did when I first saw him. I thought he had the ability as a young player to be as good as there ever was in college football, provided he learned to play with a little more mental toughness. It's hard to question how a person feels when only they know that, but he progressed. So, those were true statements, yes."

Lee Jenkins, a two-year starter at cornerback for the Vols (1981–82) and a roommate of White at UT, recalls a hilarious tale that took place on the turf of Neyland Stadium on September 19, 1981.

"We were playing Colorado State at home," recounts Jenkins, president and CEO of Jenkins Wealth Advisors, a financial planning firm in Atlanta. "He was such a great quarterback sacker. On this one play, their quarterback drops back to pass, and as soon as he releases the ball, Reggie clobbers the guy. Now, unbeknownst to Reggie, I intercept the ball and I'm running down the sidelines for a touchdown.

"Well, in the meantime, before I intercept the ball, while the ball is up in the air, Reggie's laying on the guy. He clobbers the quarterback but then helps the guy up. Well, the guy takes off and tackles me before I can score a touchdown! So, Reggie did a good thing and a bad thing on the same play. He was ferocious enough to make the sack and to cause the guy to throw an errant pass, but he was so Christian and nice that he helped the guy up, and the guy runs and tackles me on the sideline!

"That was the only time in my whole career that I had a chance to score a touchdown. I never let Reggie forget it. Every three or four times Reggie and I talked, I would say, 'Man, I can't believe you didn't—all you had to do was lay on the guy! Just lay on him two more seconds and I'm in the end zone!'

"In the huddle, on the field, it was just typical Reggie White," adds Jenkins about his teammate's larger-than-life presence, "making sacks and encouraging guys. He was a real leader. When we had to dig in, he would say, 'All right guys, come on! We gotta stop 'em.' He was the cheerleader and the leader on the field. No doubt."

Johnny Majors remembers the inherent leadership qualities evident in his prize defensive lineman as an underclassman at Tennessee. Often White would serve as a go-between spokesperson-type mediator for the players. Majors, always impressed with White's self-confidence and poise, would eye his young athlete, a known jokester, hoping to divine White's intent.

"He'd come in occasionally and say, 'Coach Majors, the players wanted me to come see you. They think practice is too long' or 'We're doing too much hitting,'" says the man who notched 116 victories over sixteen seasons as the Vols' guiding force. "I said, 'Reggie did the *players* want you to come here, or did *you* want to come here to tell me *you* thought we were doing too much hitting?' I would take him seriously, but I'd be a little lighthearted about it and always kind of put it back on his shoulders: 'You're just trying to get a lighter schedule in practice.' That kind of thing.

"We finished the 1983 season, barely getting by Vanderbilt and Kentucky," Majors says. "We weren't very good, but we got a bid to the Florida Citrus Bowl. I told our staff, 'We're gonna have a renewal of spirit around here, and we're gonna have a lot of contact between now and the bowl game. This team is not very good fundamentally, and we're gonna have a revival of football fundamentals.' So we did a lot of hitting and scrimmaging in the weeks leading up to the bowl game.

"Reggie and two or three of the guys saw me after practice one day and said, 'Coach Majors, the players think that bowl games oughta be a reward.'

"'Let me tell you something,' I said. 'There's not going to be any reward for any of you guys unless you start hitting and blocking and tackling better and playing harder-nosed football. There's not gonna be any rewards once we get there or before we get there. If you do what I ask you to do, if you get out there and hit and get better fundamentally, I'll give you rewards when we get to the bowl site.'

"But he was no malingerer; he was no loafer. When it came time to blow the whistle, Reggie White would line up there and whip any man one-on-one or be the best guy on that side of the line of scrimmage. Quite often, he would control a side of the line of scrimmage and force people to run the other way and disrupt their offense."

Raleigh McKenzie, who, along with his brother Reggie, was an acquaintance of White when all three were growing up, remembers how White would suddenly become "available" whenever the McKenzie brothers were headed to their mother's house in Knoxville on weekends.

"My parents were big Reggie White fans," says McKenzie. "They went to the same high school and grew up in his area.

When we were at Tennessee, me and my brother would try to sneak and go home, because if Reggie's looking, and if he sees us, boy, here he'd come out with a big pillowcase full of clothes, saying 'Hey man, lemme wash my clothes.' My mom had offered to him, 'Hey, whenever you want to, come on the weekends, eat, and get your clothes washed.' So Reggie would try to take advantage of it. He'd wash his before we could wash ours. It was a lot of fun, though. Reggie was a good guy."

~

McKenzie recollects the times when he and other UT friends would be in a partying mood. White was usually quick to act the part of verbal chaperone, reminding all within earshot not to take it too far.

"I still remember me and some friends of ours—like my brother and a few other football players—we were in a fraternity at Tennessee, Omega Psi Phi, and we used to throw parties," says McKenzie. "Reggie used to get on us about partying, saying we shouldn't do it. So at this one particular party we had at the Panhellenic Building [on the UT campus], there was Reggie, you know, right in the front, trying to deter us.

"There really weren't any players at the fraternity, but Reggie kind of protested our parties, so we all had to jump on him a little bit and get him off our case. But, you know, I think he understood. I think he had the wrong indication that we were going crazy, but you know, it was just music, music, and making sure everybody had a good time."

Was White policing them as a fellow football player, simply wanting his teammates to comply with training regulations, or was there a bit of the righteous in there?

"I think it was a little bit of both," McKenzie replies. "You know, he'd say stuff like, 'Hey, y'all, make sure you're not hurting the team,' from that standpoint and then from the religious, too. Of course, there's all sorts of parties in college, and I think he just felt like they all fell under that same category. And we kind of gave him a hard time. But he wasn't like that just for parties. When Reggie saw somebody doing wrong, he didn't just go into his room and lock the door, he always confronted you."

~

Coach Majors, in the classic Southern tradition of creative metaphor, found a few choice ones to describe the superior play of his All-America defensive tackle/end:

"He could pull 'em down along the line of scrimmage like a farmer shucks corn," Majors once said of White. "When you shuck corn, you shuck it fast, kind of like fingers running the piano scales. He could go right down the line of scrimmage like a pianist playing the scales on a piano."

4

Memphis

While the professional football career of Reggie White tends to make people see Philadelphia Eagles Green and Silver or Green Bay Packers Green and Gold, it was the Red, White, and Blue of the United States Football League's Memphis Showboats that first adorned White after he shed the Orange and White of the University of Tennessee. He was an immediate force in the new league, joining such future NFL notables as Herschel Walker, Jim Kelly, Steve Young, Doug Flutie, and 1983 Heisman Trophy winner Mike Rozier to play professional football in the springtime. In his rookie season of 1984, White recorded an impressive eleven sacks.

"The Memphis crowd had wanted major-league football for years and years and years," says Chuck Dickerson, White's defensive line coach with Memphis. "They had had a Continental Football League team, a World Football League team, and I think they've had several minor-league teams. When the Memphis Showboats got there—the owner was a fellow named Logan Young, a millionaire who made his money in oleomargarine, I think, in butter pats, a business that his family had—everybody really gained heart about having a professional football team. He was really Memphis.

"After Logan lost the team, we had a guy named Billy Dunavant, a cotton magnate, take over, who was very close to [FedEx mogul] Fred Smith and some of the old money in Memphis. So we had a very good base on our franchise, financially speaking. The base also came from the fans. We didn't overcharge them for tickets; they had great football. It's really a shame that the league didn't go, because the fans benefited from having a fall and a spring league."

According to White, playing in the USFL was more pure fun than the NFL because it was looser and less structured. It was also a development ground for his sensational "hump" move, the signature pass-rush technique that White made famous at future NFL stops in Philadelphia and Green Bay.

"What it was," says Dickerson, "he would attack the outside shoulder of the offensive tackle at an angle with the center of his forehead, then at the last possible moment, shift his head to the inside shoulder of the tackle and come across his shoulder with his outside arm, lifting and humping the tackle straight up in the air.

"I've seen him lift 350-pound men way off the ground," adds Dickerson, "knocking them right off their feet. I've seen him do it over and over and over again. Well, that move itself, of course, was perfected by Reggie. No one has ever done it as well, and I don't think anybody ever will. But that was John Banaszak who did that all the way with him."

Banaszak, a seven-year defensive tackle/end and three-time Super Bowl victor with the Pittsburgh Steelers, had been brought into the Showboats lineup to add stability to a young defensive front.

"Reggie and [fellow defensive lineman] Sam Clancy absolutely just adopted Banaszak," says Dickerson, who also served as the tell-it-like-it-is defensive coordinator of the Buffalo Bills' Super Bowl XXV and XXVI teams. "I had a guy named Jay Hayes, who is coaching in the NFL right now, who was with me at that time, too. These guys all became great buddies. Here are three black guys and a white guy in Memphis, Tennessee. One of them is a preacher, one of them is married with six kids, the other one is single—he liked to hit the bars. And then there's John Banaszak. Now if that isn't a combination of guys to send out into Rednecksville! They'd eat dinner and really have a good time together. They became so close that Reggie studied Banaszak a lot in practice. Banaszak had a move that he'd use that was a body club that Reggie later developed. It became his patented 'hump' move."

While the USFL had its high-profile stars to be sure, it fought an uphill fight image-wise as a second-rate league throughout its three-year existence. Pepper Rodgers, the legendary coach who guided the gridiron fortunes of UCLA, Kansas, Georgia Tech, and the Memphis Showboats, strongly disputes any inference that the spring league was inferior in any way to its long-entrenched fall rival.

"This wasn't a league of replacement players and coaches," argues Rodgers. "It was Steve Spurrier and Jack Pardee, Frank Kush, George Allen, Marv Levy, Lee Corso, Jim Mora, Lindy Infante. Fact is, half the damn head coaches in the National Football League were assistant coaches in the USFL."

The Showboats registered a major coup against the rival NFL when they landed White right out of college. In fact, White left UT early, just months shy of graduating, when he signed with the Showboats for the team's second springtime campaign, in 1984. (White would eventually return to Tennessee to complete his final classroom work, receiving his bachelor of science degree in human services in 1990.) Rodgers, while ecstatic about the fortuitous kismet that brought White to Memphis, is adamant about not taking credit for the great defensive end's meteoric development.

"I was happy he was playing for us," acknowledges Rodgers, a onetime front-office executive with both the Tennessee Oilers and Washington Redskins. "But it was like someone said to me, 'Did John Riggins play for you?' I said, 'John Riggins could play for anybody. I *recruited* him.' And I'd say the same thing about Reggie. Reggie could play for anybody. Anybody could coach him. There's no way I can say that Reggie White wouldn't have become a great pass rusher if he hadn't come to Memphis. Anybody who sits back and takes credit for making Reggie White what he is and who he is, they're whistlin' 'Dixie'!"

~

In addition to his unparalleled on-field skills, White was part showman, working the crowd like a ringmaster and reveling in its response. Calvin Clark, a Showboats defensive end and close friend of White, remembers his gifted teammate's ability to whip fans into a frenzy.

"Reggie's always the life of the party," says Clark. "There was one game where he had gotten a sack. Everybody's cheering because we made a crucial stop and we're gonna win the game. In a crazy moment, as we're trotting off the field afterward, all of a sudden he does a flip. He raises his hands up in the air, and the crowd went crazy! It just shows you the athleticism that he had. If I'd done that, I'd have woke up dizzy or I'd have hurt myself. All in this one motion of excitement, he just rolled. And that's 300-something pounds. He just rolled! He got right back up, raising his fist, and the crowd went wild."

Speaking of the crowd, Memphis had some great ones during those USFL years. Fans turned up in sailor's hats and life preservers—the Boat People. It was kind of like the Showboats' answer to Cleveland's infamous Dawg Pound. And in White, they had a superstar they could get behind.

"He played to the crowd," says Clark. "That juiced Reggie up. That got him going on the field, too. He would raise his hands up and say, 'Hey, let's get going!' He actually brought the crowd into it. He would do this before games and then during the games. It would psyche him up. He would be tired, huffing and puffing, but he would raise that fist up and the crowd would get to cheering; they'd chant his name: 'Reg-GIE! Reg-GIE! REG-*GIE!*' And he'd just come to life. He did that everywhere he went: Philadelphia, Green Bay, and he did it at Tennessee, too. He just had a knack for getting the crowd involved.

"It was like bringing another player onto the field, the way he'd charge the fans up. Then he'd go out, like Muhammad Ali, and back it up with a sack or by making a big play. He could pretty much dictate to the other team's offense what they were going to do. That's what made it so great, and then he'd get the crowd behind it. It not only juiced him up, it messed with the psyche of the opposing team. Once the crowd got to roaring, he'd go and make a play, then they *really* went wild. They felt like they were in control of him. He'd just come to life."

White's unselfishness and for-the-good-of-the-team dedication was typical standup Reggie White, as Dickerson recalls:

"We were going to a 3–4 defense, because Sam Clancy couldn't play inside and I wanted him at the defensive end," says Dickerson of the team's defensive realignment in 1985. "I didn't want to take Calvin Clark off of the field, because Calvin was really a good defensive end. My nose tackle was a kid named Brett Williams, a guy I really didn't want as a starter in a 3–4, and I didn't know how to get one of those other guys out of there if I had to keep Williams on the field.

"So, I went to Reggie, and I said, 'Reggie, this is something that I'm going to leave up to you. If you want to go to nose tackle for me, I think it's going to make us a better football team.'

"'Yes, absolutely,'" he said.

"Reggie had no reservation whatsoever about moving inside. Now, this guy's the best defensive end in football, and he immediately moves inside for me, without question, to make us a better football team. You know, there's a lot of danger in there at that nose tackle position. There's danger in every place, but more so at nose tackle because of the horrendous down blocks that you get down in there. I'll tell you, the first day he was in there, our defense became the best defense in the league. Right then. It was unbelievable."

The most celebrated event surrounding White during his years in Memphis was an infamous story involving his purchase of a rather large quantity of tube socks at a local clothing store, one that many of the players and coaches frequented. The episode generated a ton of publicity, and initially White wasn't all that sure he was happy about it. Several different takes exist on the incident.

"There was a men's clothing store in Memphis that most of the players went to," recounts Dickerson. "They had big and tall clothes in there, and everything else. Really great guys, and they took good care of our players. They gave them a good price on things. So Reggie went in there one day, and he wanted to buy some over-the-calf hose. He's talking to the salesman. He said, 'Show me the colors and different kinds.' So, the guy shows him all these different kinds of socks he's got him in there. Reggie is like, 'I like those, give me a dozen of those; I like those, give me a dozen of those. I like those, give me a dozen of those.'

"Before he gets out of there, he buys over a gross! Over a gross of over-the-calf hose! It wasn't a matter of money, because Reggie was making a pretty good salary with us. So he comes back the next day, and he says, 'Coach, I don't know what to do. I got like 200 pair of socks! Two hundred pair of socks! I went in there and they all looked so nice, I thought I'd get some for Calvin and some for Clance and some of the other guys. I ended up buying about 200 pair, maybe more than that!'

"So, I call up this place. I say: 'What do you think about this?'

"They say, 'Tell him to bring the socks back. We don't care."

"'No, no, no,' Reggie says, 'I'm going to give all these socks away.'

"We had a public relations guy with us who came up with a gimmick from all this, because it became a big deal in the paper," says Dickerson. "You know, 'Reggie White Hooked on Socks,' that kind of thing. So, the next game we played Birmingham at home, and the 'Sock Exchange' got started. All the fans brought socks, and they would roll them over their heads. With Reggie, no matter what started out good or bad, it always ended up good. Things just had a way of working themselves out that way."

Rodgers remembers the Great Sock Story this way:

"Reggie was written up in a religious magazine—and Reggie actually told this story—and it was the highlight of his mother's career, in the sense that he'd never made a religious magazine before," Rodgers begins. "What had happened was, Reggie thought he was still in college; he was making $300,000 a year, but he was thinking you could still get things for free. He went into a store to get some clothes—I'm not sure if he went to buy them or he thought the guy was going to give them to him. So, he picked out fifty pairs of socks. So, the fifty pairs of socks became a symbol for everyone in town, because the guy sent him a bill, and Reggie started crying about it, said his mother was going to be so embarrassed. Everybody started saying, 'Let's bring some socks to the game for Reggie. Reggie needs socks.' He was so embarrassed.

"We're getting ready to go out onto the field, and I said, 'Reggie, look. They've been trying to get me all my life, but you know what? They can't touch me. I just turn right around and poke fun at myself. So, here's what we're going to do. I'm going to introduce the defensive team, and they'll run through the goalposts as we go onto the field. But you're going to be the last guy out. Every one of our defensive guys is going to run out waving a sock. Then, what I want you to do—you're the last one—I'm going to give you a big wad of socks, a big stack of 'em. Then you run through the goalposts and just run around the field throwing those socks up into the stands. And, Reggie, they'll love you. They can't be mad at a guy who's having fun with himself.'

"So, Reggie told that story in that religious magazine going around, and it helped him get past a crisis in his life, if that was a crisis. But that just shows how sweet a guy Reggie was that he'd worry about something like that."

But White's take was a bit different. In an earlier autobiography co-written with Terry Hill, White claims he was blatantly taken advantage of by the clothing store's salesman.

"I had picked out just a few pairs of socks, but . . . as I emptied the sack, I found that there were more than thirty pairs in the bag. I was furious. The salesman . . . had obviously taken advantage of me and stuffed the extra socks in the bag," said White of the incident. "Upon closer examination of my sales receipt, I realized that he had charged me for every pair. Fuming, I packed up everything I had bought and rushed back to that store. I returned everything that I had bought that day."[1]

Now you know how stories based in fact become legends and myths.

Of the USFL teams, the Houston Gamblers, led by quarterback Jim Kelly, who would later guide the NFL's Buffalo Bills to four Super Bowl appearances and ultimately land in the Pro Football Hall of Fame, provided the most trouble for the Showboats. Kelly directed the Gamblers' high-scoring offense, and both Rodgers and Dickerson vividly recollect those confrontations.

"We played Jim Kelly and Jack Pardee in that Run 'n' Shoot," says Rodgers. "No matter what they did, we were coming with our big Reggie as hard as we could come on their little fullback. We were going to squash him back into the quarterback [Kelly]. You don't have to sack the quarterback, but you push the blocker back in his face. When they caught the ball, we weren't bothered, because we were going to hit 'em with so many hats that they didn't want to catch it anymore.

"So, we had Reggie getting back in the backfield; that was his No. 1 job. He would line up on the quarterback's throwing side. What you've got to do out of that Run 'n' Shoot is run an option once in a while to keep those outside linebackers honest. But what Reggie could do was, he could *run*. He had such athletic ability. Everything else was incidental. If he'd have run a 5.3 [40-yard dash time], he'd have been a strong pass rusher. But he ran probably 4.7 at 290 pounds and had all that momentum.

"The worst thing Reggie did when he first came to the pros, if you just picture this, was hitting *to*, not *through*, as a pass rusher. When you're tackling a man, you don't hit *to* him, you hit *through* him. *To*, you just stop. When you hit a golf ball, you don't hit *to*, you hit *through*. When you hit a tennis ball, you hit *through*, not *to*.

"The most important thing you can do in establishing leverage is to come out of your stance like a projectile. Never come up straight. Don't get into your stance, come up straight, and then start working your feet trying to dodge a guy. The sooner you can get to him, the quicker you can throw him away and get to the quarterback.

"When Reggie first came out, he was a stand-up guy who started dodging the tackle. You don't dodge the guy! Watch a punt return. Everybody takes off running down the field. They run *through* somebody; they don't stand there and dodge. If they stand there and dodge, somebody knocks the hell out of 'em.

"Reggie developed that skill [of hitting *through*], and I think that, with all of his great athletic ability, that's why, in a short period of time, he became the greatest pass rusher in the history of the National Football League. I know Bruce Smith broke his record, but I don't know how long it took him. Reggie played by the rules, he played hard, and he never missed a practice."

Dickerson remembers a critical situation in a game against the Gamblers that brought out the best in White and awed observers.

"It's fourth and about four, and they're near our red zone," says Dickerson. "If they get a first down, they're gonna score at least a field goal to beat us. There's a timeout, and several players come to the side. I said, 'With Kelly, you know he's gonna sprint one way or the other, so you gotta play the head of the center. Reggie, take the head of the center.' We had our defense called.

"Well, they fool us, and they run an option, a no-dive option. Reggie White makes the tackle on the far sideline versus the running back off the pitch. They don't make the first down. That game catapulted us into the playoffs. A loss in that game, as I remember, would've taken us out."

One of White's major USFL performances came against the Mouse Davis-coached Denver Gold.

"Reggie, I think, had seven sacks in that game off the nose against the Run 'n' Shoot," recollects Dickerson. "Unbelievable. Hell, they were doubling him and cutting him; they were grabbing him and tackling him. It didn't make any difference. He ate that team alive. I talked to Mouse after the game. He says, 'Having that guy on the nose, my God, there's nothing you can do about that guy!' There've been just so many games where Reggie did incredible things like that."

No question, White was a handful for opponents. His skills were so predominant that teams facing him over-corrected, more often than not leaving the door wide open for White's teammates to make plays.

"The thing that set Reggie apart," Dickerson says, "aside from the great talent and strength and everything he had, was that he separated from a block to the ball faster than any big man I have ever seen in my entire life. I have coached the two greatest defensive ends in the history of the game [Bruce Smith being the other]. Nobody else who has ever been a position coach has done that. The two greatest ever. And I promise you, there's never been a player who could separate from initial contact and get to the ball laterally faster than Reggie

White. This guy was something. He was so special. When I saw film on him from Tennessee when we were looking at drafting him, I said, 'My God.' I couldn't believe it. I couldn't believe it.

"You know what Reggie did?" Dickerson continues. "He put so much fear into offensive coordinators' game plans, into their heart and into their head, that they would make adjustments in game plans all week when they were facing Reggie White. That wasn't just in Memphis, it was true in every place he's ever been. And they made the key mistake that most people make: creating vast changes to try to overcome one guy, thus weakening yourself some place else structurally. I saw that over and over and over and over.

"It didn't take us long in a game with Reggie to figure out what the other team's scheme was going to be, their pass-rush scheme. So we moved him all over the place. You're not going to take him out of a game, no matter what they do."

Dickerson and White both loved working for the colorful Rodgers, an impassioned yet carefree and fun-loving personality whose coaching fortunes had taken him across the country to three major universities, before he signed on with the Showboats. When the USFL folded after the 1985 season, Rodgers went to work in the NFL for the front offices of the Tennessee Oilers and later the Washington Redskins. He was the 1954 Sugar Bowl MVP as a left-handed throwing quarterback for the Ramblin' Wreck of Georgia Tech and once modeled his left-handed jump pass after a Tech icon of the 1940s, the legendary Clint Castleberry.

"Everything about Coach Rodgers was laid-back—his wildly mismatched clothes, his unruly hair, and his shoes worn without socks," White once said of his coach in Memphis.[2] "He had a laid-back way of talking, a laid-back way of coaching, and a friendly, inspiring style of motivating his players, which contrasted with the loud, raucous, and even abusive style of many other coaches."

Dickerson recalls that the repartee between Rodgers and White sometimes created the impression the two were a comedy team.

"Pepper had a great sense of humor, and he loved to mess around with Reggie," says Dickerson. "When you got those two guys together, they kept you mesmerized all afternoon. I can remember one day we were in the office and Reggie came in there. Pepper never wore socks; he was into the Gucci loafers and no socks. Reggie tells him, 'Coach, I'm really sorry! You know, when I had all those socks, I forgot to give you a pair.' That went on all the time. And, of course, Pepper would come back with some equally sharp barb. What better guy for Reggie White to have started his pro career with than Pepper Rodgers? Pepper loved life, too.

"He and Reggie, they would battle philosophies all the time," Dickerson adds. "I remember one fight they got into about Reggie being all worried about something he had done in a game. Reggie said, 'You know, I'm a role model for young kids.' Well, Pepper jumped all over that: 'You're a role model for a guy who can't tackle or can't rush the passer.' It was kind of one of those tongue-in-cheek deals that they would get into. I'm telling you, I was laughing so hard, tears were in my eyes. It was really funny."

As far as Dickerson's own relationship with his head coach, he says he couldn't have had it any better.

"It was great to work with and for Pepper," he says, "because Pepper let you do your thing. He hired you because of your expertise, and he fired you if you weren't any good. What else could you ask for?"

Rodgers not only had a high regard for White's athletic abilities, but he valued his star's sense of team play as well. On the field, during practice sessions with the Showboats, Rodgers used to have the squad practice two bizarre "plays" designed to promote team unity, and, well, inestimable regard for their coach.

"One of the things that I have a difficult time with in football is when someone catches a touchdown pass and acts like he did it on his own," confesses Rodgers. "When you hit a home run, you hit it by yourself. But when you score a touchdown . . . So, I would put a team out on the field by themselves on Fridays before the games. I would have the quarterback drop back and throw a long touchdown pass down the field to a receiver. That receiver would catch that ball, and then I'd make him stand in the end zone, holding that ball up until everybody touched it—because the receiver is no more important than the left tackle, the left guard, the center, the right guard, or the rest of the guys.

"And then, we'd practice 'coach carrying.' I would always make Reggie carry me, because he was the biggest-tallest, and I wanted any alumni around to look up there and say, 'You know, Pepper might not be much of a coach, but the players sure love him.'"

Rodgers continues, commenting on White's exceptional athleticism for a big man, and how he came to play for the Showboats.

"I watched him before practice, and he'd get out and play touch football with the backs," says Rodgers. "He could run and he could catch a ball. An interesting side thing on Reggie: he played harder and better football without having a mean bone in his body. He knew how to separate being a good person from being a football player.

"When Reggie was signed by us, he was obviously one of

the top players in the country. Now how did we get Reggie White? Obviously we paid him some money, but it wasn't like what they're paying guys now. One of the key guys in helping us get Reggie was a student at UT, where Reggie played. His daddy was a dentist over in Memphis, and the kid and Reggie were close friends. This guy worked in the equipment room at UT, handing out socks and jocks. That's how Reggie knew him.

"This guy helped us and gave us information on what Reggie liked and didn't like—it was a recruiting job, as well as money, but more of a recruiting job, making him [Reggie] feel comfortable, seeing if he wanted to play in Memphis. Reggie had an agent, but later, after Reggie went up to Philadelphia, he fired that agent and then hired this guy that had been the equipment guy and his friend over at UT. That man today is Jimmy Sexton, now one of the hot agents out there. Back then, Jimmy hooked up with Kyle Rote Jr. Signing Reggie was their first biggie. They [Sexton and Rote] have three or four guys over here with the Redskins. He's one of the biggies now."

Calvin Clark reflects on those precious days in Memphis and the opportunity he had to play with fabulous players and coaches:

"It was great; it was all great," says Clark. "Chuck [Dickerson] would do things to fire us up; he had a little fire behind him. Pepper Rodgers was as loose as they came; he was full of exhortation. And Reggie just fit right in with that. We all fed off of it, literally, especially as a defense. It was just a fun, fun time to play. And, of course, Reggie was young; Walter Lewis [Showboats quarterback] was young—they were sort of like the team's franchise players.

"There were so many expectations put upon those guys, but they both went out and fulfilled them. They really got the crowd behind the Memphis Showboats, and it was exciting. It was fun to come watch us play. You got to see Reggie White on defense, with his athleticism, and then you got to watch Walter Lewis on the other side, with his athleticism. It always kept the crowd excited."

5

Philadelphia

While successfully inaugurating his pro football career with the Memphis Showboats in the spring seasons of 1984 and '85, Reggie White became the fourth overall selection in the 1984 NFL Supplemental Draft, taken by the Philadelphia Eagles.

White's years in Philadelphia were highlighted by the presence of Buddy Ryan as head coach. The ex-defensive coordinator for the 1985 Super Bowl champion Chicago Bears and architect of its renowned and much-copied 46 defense, Ryan took over the Eagles' reigns in 1986, White's second season with the club. The Philly head man's initial assessment of his star defensive end's talent was prophetic:

"I've been around a lot of great defensive linemen, and Reggie's the best I've ever been around," said Ryan. "He's got better mobility than any of them. I think he's not only going to be good, I think he's going to dominate the game."[1]

Ryan's comments came without the benefit of ever having seen White play in a game, just in practice. To gauge the impact of Ryan's words, consider that he had coached several notable All-Pro and Hall of Fame linemen in earlier stints as an assistant, not only with Chicago, where he personally mentored Dan Hampton (inducted into the Pro Football Hall of Fame in 2002) and Richard Dent (a consistent high finisher in Hall of Fame balloting), but also with Minnesota, from 1969 to 1971, where he tutored HOFers Carl Eller and Alan Page, not to mention the great Jim Marshall, who should be in the Hall.

White was flattered by the remark but not quite sure how to take it. "To this day," he said years later, "I don't know if Buddy was trying to motivate me or humble me, but those words blew through me like a cool breeze, creating a bond of respect and appreciation that I feel for Coach Ryan to this day. I also took that compliment as a challenge to be worthy of the praise, and I worked harder for that man than for any other coach I had ever played for up to that time."[2]

For White, the Eagles era quickly crystallized into a dominating display of a young player with promising ability gone totally wild. Like a hungry lion, White immediately made a dramatic impact on the Philadelphia defense, debuting against the New York Giants on September 29, 1985, with a 2.5-sack performance. In that same game, he deflected a pass that was intercepted by Herman Edwards and returned for a touchdown. By year's end, White had been named to the league's all-rookie team and was selected NFC Defensive Rookie of the Year by the NFL Players Association.

In just his second year in the league, concluding the 1986 season, White went to his first Pro Bowl, and what an auspicious appearance it was. He established a Pro Bowl record for most sacks, with four, and for that command performance was named the all-star game's MVP.

The following year, the strike-shortened '87 season, White was a unanimous All-Pro selection for the first time in his fifteen NFL seasons. In all, he would receive that honor seven times during his career. Had he the benefit of playing a full sixteen-game slate in 1987, it is academic that White, with an astronomical twenty-one sacks in just twelve games, would have broken New York Jets defensive end Mark Gastineau's all-time NFL single-season sack record of twenty-two.

That same year, during a 34–24 loss to the Redskins in the season opener at Washington, White scored the one and only touchdown of his NFL career, on a seventy-yard strip-and-return. To say it was one of the highlights of his lengthy pro career would be a reckless understatement.

The game began with White nailing Redskins starting quarterback Jay Schroeder on a passing down. The QB landed hard on his right shoulder and one play later left the game for good. Washington then trotted out backup QB Doug Williams, the former field general with the Tampa Bay Buccaneers, onto the turf at RFK Stadium. It would be a harbinger of good things to come for Washington. Williams never relinquished the starter's spot again en route to experiencing his career season in the sun, as he guided Washington to a climactic victory that year in Super Bowl XXVI.

Minutes before the half, White got clocked by a Redskins double team and lay on the ground for several moments. The Washington faithful rejoiced, applauding the fallen defender now on his back. White said that while he took a shot, he wasn't seriously hurt, and that the rude fan reaction only served to ignite him. With just eight seconds left in the third quarter, the Minister of Defense got his redemption.

With the Eagles trailing, 24–17, Washington's Williams retreated to pass. White blew by his man and barreled into the passer's blind side just as Williams was about to release the ball. The impact caused Williams's arm to extend, and as

Photo courtesy of David and Helen Bowman private collection

Philadelphia's defensive front, 1987–91: top, from left, White and Mike Golic; bottom, from left, Mike Pitts, Clyde Simmons, and Jerome Brown.

White noted, there was the ball right in front of him! He snatched the ball out of the Redskins quarterback's hand and raced seventy yards for the game-tying TD. Several seconds later, in the end zone, White spotted his wife, Sara, pregnant at the time, in the first row of seats and nearly hurdled them in his excitement.

The tally was White's second touchdown of his pro career, having found the end zone once with the Memphis Showboats on a thirty-yard run on a fumble return against Birmingham.

White's heady elation was short-lived, as Washington returned the ensuing kickoff fifty-four yards, with Williams quickly connecting on a thirty-nine-yard scoring aerial to Art Monk on the first play from scrimmage. The Redskins topped it off with a closing field goal for the final margin.

A former teammate of White at the University of Tennessee, Raleigh McKenzie, an offensive lineman with Washington for ten seasons of his sixteen-year NFL career, was on the field at RFK that afternoon and recalls what it was like to see his old friend lined up on the opposite side:

"With the Buddy Ryan defense, Reggie played a lot over center, and then when I did play center, I got to play against him a handful of times," says McKenzie, who followed White to both Philadelphia and Green Bay in later years but never when White was there. "Luckily enough, I held my own. Every game we played, he was like, 'Man, I just want to get one sack over you, just one! Next time, you better come with *something*, because I'm gonna get you!'"

McKenzie remembers the time when he presented the only obstacle to what would have been his old friend's second NFL touchdown. Chronologically, the event referred to by McKenzie preceded White's seventy-yarder in '87.

"I swear, if he was living today, he would still be mad at me for that time when we were in Philadelphia," McKenzie says. "He sacked the quarterback, picked up the fumble, and was about twenty yards from a touchdown. He was going down the sideline, and I caught him and knocked him out of bounds at about the 10-yard line. He got up, and I think that's probably the most mad I've ever seen him.

"'I can't believe it! You could have let me score!'

"They were killing us that game," McKenzie adds. "It wouldn't have mattered if they got another touchdown. He would still tease me about it. He did so many good things. He did end up scoring that touchdown against us up at RFK, so he got his touchdown. He had to run a little longer there. I couldn't catch him."

For White, the seventy yards to the goal line in the '87 game against Washington seemed like a distant object on the horizon. "I couldn't believe how far it was," he said. "You see, defensive linemen don't get to become running backs very often. It looked as if a touchdown was at least a mile away. To a 285-pound defensive lineman, those seventy yards might as well have been two miles."[3]

In 1988, for the second straight year, White led the league in sacks, with eighteen. On September 25, at Minnesota, he recorded the third four-sack game of his career and at season's end was tabbed as the NFL Player of the Year by the Washington Touchdown Club.

Two years later, on *Monday Night Football*, he intercepted his first NFL pass, courtesy of Redskins quarterback Jeff Rutledge in a game against Washington, returning the deflected aerial thirty-three yards. In that same 1990 campaign, on December 16, this time against his future employer, the Green Bay Packers, White created holy havoc, almost single-handedly skinning the Pack with 1.5 sacks, six knockdowns, two passes batted at the line, and a forced fumble in a 31–0 romp. The Packer tackle victimized by White that day was the oft-maligned Tony Mandarich, the former No. 2 overall pick in the 1989 draft. This is how the ordeal appeared to him:

"To tell you the truth, I gave it my damnedest," Mandarich said after the game. "He timed my step and then he'd toss me. I could have held onto him, but why hold? Why go back ten yards?"[4]

The 1991 season was all of one quarter old when new Eagles head coach Rich Kotite's debut season was effectively scuttled. On the first play of the second quarter of the season opener against Green Bay, Packers linebacker Bryce Paup barreled into Philadelphia quarterback Randall Cunningham, sending the signal caller to the sideline with two torn knee ligaments. Cunningham would not see action for the remainder of the season.

Despite the loss on offense of the team's top QB, it would be a bellwether year for the Eagles' defensive front. In that first game in Green Bay, White registered one of his biggest career performances, recording three quarterback sacks, forcing two fumbles (one of which he recovered), and batting a pass that was intercepted by line mate Mike Golic.

"He tipped it, and I intercepted it," says Golic, White's teammate of six years in Philadelphia (1987–92). "He decided to block the wrong guy so I couldn't score."

Uhh, say that again?

"Oh, I know deep down inside he did it on purpose," Golic maintains. "Don Majkowski was the quarterback. Reggie tipped the pass, and I intercepted it. Reggie was right behind me; to the right of me was an offensive lineman; and behind us both was Majkowski. All Reggie had to do was turn around and block the quarterback. I could have outrun the offensive lineman, but Reggie decided to block the lineman, who I didn't need blocked, and let the quarterback run and trip me up from behind.

"I remember, after the game, a reporter asked me about it. I made it out like Reggie didn't want me to score, that he would have been so offended if I scored that he decided not to block the guy that was going to make the tackle. We had a lot of fun with that one, back and forth—people trying to block for other people. I had three interceptions in my career, and the quarterback tackled me every time. Reggie never failed to give me grief about that."

Though the Eagles went on to win that game over Green Bay, 20–3, a second straight 10–6 regular season gained them no better than a third-place finish in the NFC East. In the course of the season, a poll conducted by CBS Sports asked NFL general managers to name one player from the league around which, if they had their choice, they would build their defense. White's name was selected more than any other.

In addition, three of the Eagles' defensive linemen—White, Jerome Brown, and Clyde Simmons—all made first team All-Pro and all three started for the NFC in that year's Pro Bowl. That marked the first time in ten years that three defensive linemen from the same team had been so honored and only the sixth time in NFL history that such a rarity had occurred. Matching the feat were the 1967 Los Angeles Rams (Merlin Olsen, Deacon Jones, Roger Brown), 1974 Pittsburgh Steelers (Mean Joe Greene, L. C. Greenwood, Dwight White), 1975 Rams (Olsen, Fred Dryer, Jack Youngblood), and the 1981 San Diego Chargers (Fred Dean, Louie Kelcher, Gary Johnson). In 1969, the Minnesota Vikings became the only team in NFL history to send four defensive linemen to the Pro Bowl (Alan Page, Carl Eller, Jim Marshall, Gary Larsen).

The accolades didn't stop there. The Philadelphia defense achieved a rare triple statistically, ending the season ranked No. 1 in the league in rushing defense, passing defense, and yards allowed. White personally added another laurel to his growing collection when he was named NFL Defensive Player of the Year by *Pro Football Weekly*.

"With all of Reggie's great years, it's tough to pinpoint one as the best, but he probably had his top season [with us] in 1991," says Dale Haupt, White's defensive line coach in Philadelphia. "He was a great football player. I had three All-Pro guys there in Philly: Reggie, Jerome Brown, and Clyde Simmons."

Haupt couldn't help but compare White to another Hall of Famer he'd worked with in Chicago, the Bears' Dan Hampton.

"Reggie was much heavier," says Haupt, now retired and living on his farm in South Carolina. "They were about the same size. Dan was about 6–5, 265. They both could play inside—tackle—and outside. In our 46 defense, one of the ends had to move down over the guard. Both of them could do about the same. Dan was a great football player, and Reggie, of course, was a great football player, too. Reggie didn't have any injuries; he was solid."

Hampton, known as "Danimal," wasn't so fortunate, health-wise, during his twelve years in the league, all with Chicago. The courageous Hall of Famer underwent twelve knee operations over the course of his career. White, on the other hand, never encountered a debilitating injury nor required any knee surgery during his seventeen-year professional career, including his two years in the USFL.

Haupt recalls that every Monday during football season, normally a day off for players, he would receive a phone call from an anxious White.

"Most of the time he'd call me," says Haupt. "'Hey, Coach, how'd I do? How many tackles did I get? How many assists? Did they give me a sack on that one?' All the players are like that. He was very conscientious about his performance. He liked to have fun, too, though. He would mess around out on the practice field sometimes. But most of the time he was dead serious."

Haupt believes a minor campaign of sorts needs to be mounted to remind people that White was an Eagle. "I coached for seven years [at Philadelphia]. Peter Giunta [defensive and special teams assistant with Philadelphia while Haupt was with the Eagles] says everybody, when they talk about Reggie White, they always think of the Green Bay Packers, which is wrong. Sure he went to the Super Bowl with them and made it to the Pro Bowl, things like that, but he was the defensive Most Valuable Player [a consensus pick once each in Philadelphia and Green Bay]. He played eight years for us at Philadelphia; he didn't play that long with Green Bay [seven seasons]. They don't ever think of Reggie playing for Philadelphia."

Fellow defensive end and two-time Pro Bowler Clyde Simmons, White's teammate for seven years with the Eagles, and as previously mentioned, part of one of the great lines in NFL history, with White and Jerome Brown, talks about the special season of 1991, the year in which all three defensive linemen made All-Pro and started in the Pro Bowl.

"It was pretty special," acknowledges Simmons. "We all fed off of each other. We were a pretty good team, in that we had a lot of great players on the team—not just defensive linemen, both offensive and defensive players—where we'd set off each other. I guess we all inspired each other to be better. When you go about handling things and those aspects, I think it makes you better as a whole."

Chuck Dickerson, defensive coordinator of the USFL's Memphis Showboats and later architect of the Bills' Super Bowl-era defenses in Buffalo, recalls meeting White one time at the Pro Bowl in Honolulu and having an interesting conversation with his former pupil and standout, who then made a surprising request of Dickerson.

PHOTO COURTESY OF DAVID AND HELEN BOWMAN PRIVATE COLLECTION

White and Philadelphia Eagles defensive line mates Clyde Simmons (96) and Jerome Brown (99) with defensive line coach Dale Haupt.

"When I was with the Bills, we were coaching the Pro-Bowl," Dickerson remembers. "The Bills' staff and I were part of the AFC, and Reggie was there to represent the NFC. I can't remember if it was '90 or '91 . . . '89 . . . Anyway, he called me before we went over to Hawaii. He said, 'If we get an opportunity to see each other, boy, I'm really looking forward to it. I got some things I really want to talk to you about.'

"I said, 'Sure Reggie, anytime.' We talked frequently. I mean, we were close. So we got over there, he and Sara, and my wife, Shirley, and myself, and we all went to lunch. He said, 'Coach, have you got time to come up to my room?'

"I said, 'Sure, let's go on up. What do you want to talk about?'

"He said, 'Well, I don't want to talk about it down here.'

"So, we went up to his room. And he said, 'You know, I'm really having trouble with my swat'—a pass-rush move. So we end up in his suite—the penthouse of this hotel we were in, working on pass-rush moves up there. Now, I'm coaching with the Buffalo Bills and he's with the Philadelphia Eagles, for crying out loud! He said, 'Now, don't say anything to anybody!'

"I said, 'I won't say anything.' Because I knew he'd get into trouble if I did. So when we left, he said, 'Do you mind if from time to time I send you my game film? Look it over and get back to me and see what you think.'

"So, from that point on, while I was with the Bills, Reggie sent me a weekly game film," says Dickerson. "I evaluated him, and when he went on to Green Bay, I continued to do the same thing. It wasn't that he didn't listen to his coaches. That wasn't it at all. He was a very coachable guy. But here was a guy that wanted to learn everything he could from anybody that he felt comfortable with, who had the expertise to help him. I always thought that was kind of a real feather in his hat: to be able to listen to other people, because by then, there was no question about him being the best football player in the league at his position."

~

All of the Eagles were almost like fans when it came to the appreciation of White's unparalleled football skills. Wide receiver Mike Quick, White's teammate for six years, from 1985 to 1990, remembers an instance where White utilized his prodigious strength to send a message to one unfortunate offensive lineman.

"I can't remember who we were playing," says Quick, a five-time Pro Bowler. "But, I remember that when Reggie came off the field, he was a bit upset. So, I made sure I watched him when he went back onto the field. The very next play, or maybe it was just after that, he takes the offensive tackle with one arm, and he just tosses him to the side. I mean, the offensive tackle is a 320-pound guy, and he just tossed him to the side and went after the quarterback.

"He perfected what they call the 'hump' move. It was Reggie's deal. I don't know anybody who was doing it before Reggie. But that's what he would do: with one arm, he would just take one of those big 300-pound guys and toss them to the side on his way to the quarterback."

One of the strangest games during White's tenure in Philadelphia was the 1988 NFC Divisional Playoff contest against the Chicago Bears on the afternoon of New Year's Eve, better known as the Fog Bowl.

The Buddy Ryan-led Eagles came into the fray as NFC East champions but with a moderate 10–6 record, remarkable in the fact that Philly was headed for a losing season before winning nine of its last twelve games. But what developed in the playoff game at times seemed surreal, as ghostly figures negotiated the misty shroud of dank Soldier Field.

The first half of the game was played in sunshine, but then, late in the second quarter, a dense fog rolled in, which White likened to a blanket of thick smoke from a forest fire.

"At times, visibility was only ten to fifteen yards," said White, "and the football was just a faint blur. . . . At one point in the game, referee Jim Tunney—the official who made the decision to keep playing—came into the Eagles huddle. He asked Randall [Cunningham, Eagles quarterback], 'Can you see the goalposts at the other end?' Randall looked downfield and saw nothing but a wall of gray. 'Nope,' he said. Then

Tunney said, 'Can you see the thirty-second clock?' Again, Randall said, 'Nope.' Tunney shrugged and said, 'Well, don't worry about a delay-of-game penalty. We won't call it today.'"[5]

The bizarre conditions, limited the Eagles to just four Luis Zendejas field goals, though Philadelphia logged more first downs than did Chicago, twenty-two to fourteen, and was inside or on the Bears' 25-yard line nine out of its thirteen offensive possessions.

"But the deal is, both teams had to play in it," says Mike Golic, a Fog Bowl participant. "They [the officials] weren't going to call it. There's no way they were going to send all those people home and try to do it another day. The funniest thing to me was the referee standing in the middle of the field, and I heard him say on his microphone, 'Yes, I can still see both goal posts from the middle of the field.' I'm looking both ways thinking, *What the hell are you talking about?*

"They kept in constant contact with the ref, because from the press box you couldn't see. You couldn't see ten yards. There would be a sweep, and the guy would go out of vision. It basically was whoever was winning when the fog rolled in was going to win that game. They [Chicago] had the lead when it rolled in. It was amazing how it engulfed the field. But it was an experience."

In an account of the game in the *New York Times*, writer Frank Litsky noted that "the public address announcer at Soldier Field couldn't see what was happening. So an aide relayed the plays to the press box by walkie-talkie. 'This is the best game I've never seen,' said one upper deck spectator."

Cunningham, despite the major atmospheric obstacle, threw for an amazing 407 yards in the game but was picked three times and scored no touchdowns. "There were times I couldn't even see their safeties line up," said Cunningham of the murky veil. "We had to change our passing game because we couldn't see beyond twenty yards. We had to change to short passes, and the Bears knew it."

Eagles punt returner Gregg Garrity said that returning the two Bears punts in the game was a nightmare of uncertainty. "You couldn't see the ball until it started coming down through the fog. I've never seen anything like this before."

An NFL spokesman, Joe Browne, said that no game in NFL history had ever been cancelled before because of fog. Bears offensive guard Tom Thayer quipped, "The fog was so bad that I was waiting for Boris Karloff to come out of the stands."

Litsky noted that the game's appearance on television had "the grainy quality of a Western movie from the 1930s," and later said the TV images of the game being broadcast "looked like an old newsreel." He mentioned that one writer ultimately vacated the press box for a better vantage point from the Bears' bench because "it was like watching radio."[6]

Bears All-Pro middle linebacker Mike Singletary, a future Hall of Famer, put the game in common-sense perspective from a players' standpoint. "Probably the best thing to come from this," he said, "is that next week we won't have to see film of the game."

Eagles wideout Mike Quick, who caught five passes for eighty-two yards that afternoon, recalls the tenor of that peculiar game and the eerie specter of "half players."

"Early in the game, it wasn't a factor," says Quick. "But then the fog did roll in, and you just couldn't see. As a receiver, you go down the field for a pass, you get down the field fifteen yards, and you look back and you really can't find your quarterback. You look back, and you may be able to see the bottom half of the guys, but you couldn't really see the top half, 'cause of all the fog.

"The problem was that our real strength was throwing the football. We had Keith Jackson, we had Cris Carter, Keith

Byars, and Randall, of course. We threw the ball on offense, and that really limited what we could do when that fog came in. The strange thing is, when we came out of the locker room after we'd showered, the fog had lifted and it was a perfectly clear day."

And with the secession of the problematic fog and the eventual 20–12 loss to the Bears also went one of Philadelphia's best shots at getting to the Super Bowl. "That, I felt, was our year, during Buddy's tenure," says Quick. "Actually, during my career, that was our best opportunity to get to the Super Bowl. We had all the pieces that year [1988], but it wasn't meant to be. Everything else we had in our favor. I don't see it any other way."

The run of three years, 1988 through 1990, was Philadelphia's window of opportunity for grabbing the brass ring, make that diamond-studded ring. Buddy Ryan's team, so brimming with talent everywhere in the lineup, would exit from postseason play each year in their opening playoff round.

Clyde Simmons, too, feels the missed chances from that time, a period that ultimately sealed the fate of Ryan as Eagles head coach after the 1990 season.

"Oh yeah, we felt we were better," says Simmons. "The problem that we always had with the playoffs was that we always went in there limping. Someone would get hurt on offense or defense. It would be something freakish that would cause the season to end on a funky note. We always went in there somehow banged up on offense or banged up on defense. You can't really perform at your best level unless you're clicking on all cylinders."

The Philadelphia defense during that time was one of the great ones to many followers, but Golic, now co-host of *Mike and Mike in the Morning* on ESPN Radio, says it lacked the key ingredient.

"I got there [Philadelphia] in 1987," he says. "So many people will talk about the greatest defenses of all time on my radio show: the Pittsburgh defense, or the Baltimore defense. People write me e-mails saying, 'Why don't you mention your Eagles defense?' I say, 'Because we didn't win anything!' I say, 'You have to be able to close the deal. You can't be out in the first round of playoffs and then have the reputation of having the greatest defense ever.'

"We had a great defense, don't get me wrong. In one year we were the number-one defense in everything, and then probably during a three-year stretch we were the best defense going. But we could never close the deal.

"Now a lot of people say that year in 1991 we went through, what, seven or eight different quarterbacks? The offense really struggled," Golic adds. "But still, push comes to shove, it's a team thing. We needed to get it done. We needed some kind of hardware to justify saying the defense was one of the greatest ever, and we weren't able to do that."

After the 1991 season, White commented, "I'm still trying to get to the next level. I still think I have another gear. It's just something that has to be worked at. My game can go higher, and I know I can make it go higher."[7]

He was correct in his assessment. After finishing his eighth and final season in Philadelphia, in 1992, White departed as the Eagles' all-time leader in sacks, with 124. His *pièce de résistance* took place in 1987, when he recorded twenty-one sacks, a career best, in a strike-shortened twelve-game season.

After another Pro Bowl season in 1992, White's seventh in a row, an Eagles franchise record, he was in transition as a player. His struggles with Philadelphia owner Norman Braman were well documented. In short, a complete collapse occurred on White's part with regard to the club. Contract squabbles beginning as early as 1987, ironically which coincided with the players' strike, contributed to the eventual deterioration of White's relationship with the Eagles' front office, though he was eventually re-signed through the '92 season.

Braman apparently showed little appreciation for his star defensive end's talents. During White's lengthy negotiations with the club in 1987 and '88, the Eagles owner inferred that his perennial all-star had no right to ask for better money since he was not among the leading defensive players in the NFL, a slight that infuriated White. Completely to the contrary, White was being hailed by everyone, from reporters to team general managers, as the top defensive player in the league.

Though the league's long-standing anti-trust status with regard to player signings, virtually enslaving a player to a team through the lifetime of that player, was in the process of being torn down by a series of lawsuits and court rulings in favor of the players, White's participation as the lead plaintiff in a landmark class-action suit involving hundreds of other NFL players against the league in 1992 opened up, eventually through collective bargaining, what is now known as unrestricted free agency. Translation: freedom!

White's original intent was to stay with Philadelphia if the price was right and if the team's management showed a committed dedication to winning—elements that had not willfully surfaced during previous negotiations.

Devoted Philadelphians begged for their defensive star to stay. Almost acting in vigil, Eagles fans convened in Love Park to air pleas for White to remain in Philly. Scores of gatherers got on the microphone one at a time to add their entreaties, some with tears in their eyes, claimed one anonymous witness.

But White saw the seams beginning to split. The team that had come so far to get so close was beginning to break up, with All-Pro tight end and good friend Keith Jackson already off to Miami and the inspirational Jerome Brown gone in a fatal car accident.

It was time to move on. The well-publicized "Reggie White Tour" of the NFL was about to crank up.

6

Green Bay

I doubt that Reggie White himself ever would have believed it, but it's no myth: The NFL's No. 1 free agent prospect of 1993 wound up in Green Bay, Wisconsin, because he whupped Brett Favre's butt. But we're getting a bit ahead of ourselves.

With a clear road suddenly before him, and with his Eagles days plainly behind him, White set out hunting a new employer under circumstances that he previously only could have dreamed of. Thanks to the NFL Players Association's new collective bargaining agreement with the league owners, White now held all the cards. The slave had turned the tables on the master. NFL clubs were lining up for his services, all wanting the greatest defensive player in the game to play for them. For White, it was finally an opportunity to align with a franchise that viewed the game the same way he did, that was committed to the goal of seeking a world championship.

The offers poured in: Cleveland, Atlanta, Washington, Detroit, San Francisco. Each town and each team rolled out the red carpet for White and his wife. Lavish suites and sumptuous dinners. Every club was on its best behavior. Word apparently had even filtered out to the Cleveland organization and its then-owner, Art Modell, that there was to be no swearing or use of off-color language when White visited the team's training complex in Berea, Ohio. Such was the attention given to even the most minute details, as teams courted the Minister of Defense, hoping their town would be the place where White would ultimately unpack his bags.

As White was often wont to say, "God spoke to me, and He said . . . " Well, in this case, initially, the Supreme Being did not so much as even lightly whisper Green Bay, Wisconsin. In fact, White claimed, Divine Providence appeared to be directing him toward San Francisco, a franchise with a storied tradition and an unquestioned contender for the Super Bowl year in and year out.

While the Eagles of White's eight-year era in Philadelphia went winless against the 49ers in four tries, it now looked in all likelihood that White would take the field as a Niner for the upcoming 1993 season and assure himself of a shot at his long-awaited dream of a Super Bowl ring.

But White's agent, Jimmy Sexton, kept urging him to check out Green Bay on "The Tour." Alongside his agent's insistence to visit the tiny Wisconsin hamlet with the hallowed NFL tradition, White also began to recollect a special game still fresh in his memory from just several months earlier, in mid-November 1992, in what was to be his final season with the Eagles. And as it so happens, it was the same game in which the aforementioned can of whup-ass was opened up on a young, talented, second-year quarterback with a future Hall of Fame upside.

The contest had pitted the Eagles against the Packers at Milwaukee County Stadium. Nothing much was expected from the Pack, sitting at 3–6 for the year, while Philadelphia entered the game with just the reverse season record, at 6–3. The hometown underdogs were led by their promising quarterback from Kiln, Mississippi, starting just his seventh game in the league. Brett Favre had come to Green Bay from Atlanta after the 1991 season, via a trade generated by then-Packers General Manager Ron Wolf, a move that was highly criticized at the time. White wasted little time introducing himself and his seven-time Pro Bowl reputation to the young QB.

On Green Bay's first play of its second possession of the game, Favre retreated then completed an eleven-yard swing pass to fullback Harry Sydney. As he released the ball, Eagles defensive tackle Andy Harmon tackled Favre around the ankles, while White leveled him high. Favre fell heavily on his left side with White on top of him. The young signal caller's shoulder was instantly separated, but the gritty kid stayed in the game. By halftime, Favre could make no movement with the shoulder. A shot enabled him to continue—maimed and grimacing with every snap of the ball. The gutsy QB not only played the entire game, he produced big-time, guiding Green Bay to a 27–24 upset win, in what would be the first victory of a six-game winning streak for the Packers. That day a leader was born in Green Bay.

"After the game," said Favre, "Ron Wolf told reporters, 'Your quarterback has to be your leader. In time, this locker room will be Favre's locker room, and in time, this team will be his team.'"[1]

White never forgot Favre's courageous and skillful performance under such extremely painful circumstances. Favre said outright that White's shot was the hardest hit of his athletic career. His shoulder was damaged to the extent that he couldn't tie his shoes, put on a coat, or even drive a car. The injury troubled Favre for the remainder of the season, but he never missed a start.[2]

When White finally arrived in Green Bay on the Upper Midwest leg of the Reggie Tour, he had lunch with Favre and told him that his courage that day had impressed him. That impression would become an important cornerstone in fashioning White's final choice of where to play football, now that he was free to sign with any team. As White would later state upon inking with Green Bay, Favre's physical and mental toughness, not to mention his obvious on-field abilities displayed that November 15 afternoon, played a significant part in his eventual decision.

Green Bay's style of courting the much sought-after free agent went something like this: instead of the usual five-star restaurant treatment, the Packers escorted Reggie to Red Lobster so that he might order catfish, his favorite meal. Ray Rhodes, Green Bay's defensive coordinator at the time, also played a major role in landing White. On one occasion, Rhodes, along with then-head coach Mike Holmgren, unexpectedly turned up in Knoxville, where White was then living, to attend a function where Reggie was scheduled to speak. Their appearance both shocked and impressed White.[3]

There is little doubt, though, it was Holmgren's phone call that sealed the deal that brought White to the Packers. In what became an instant classic, the coach at one point reportedly left a voice-mail message on White's phone, simply saying, "This is God calling. Come to Green Bay." White had publicly stated that he would consider going to the tiny Midwest town if he felt God was calling him there.

Former *Green Bay Press-Gazette* writer Tony Walter, now the paper's assistant metro editor, was there when White finally put his name on a Packers contract. The signing of the giant free agent prize created terrific PR for Green Bay.

"I remember [my reaction] when the Packers announced that Reggie was signing here," says Walter. "It was, 'Oh wow!'

It put the Packers on the NFL map. Nobody really expected that. We knew that he had come through here and had, in a sense, spent some time with Brett Favre. It was just, you know, an impact. I remember going to the press conference; he was there with Mike Holmgren and Ron Wolf in the Packers locker room. It was just a monumental moment in the history of the franchise. That and the Favre trade.

"I've seen some statistics that, since 1992, the Packers are the winningest team in the National Football League. They've won more games than any other program. Favre in '92, then Reggie in '93. It was pivotal. That press conference was just a dramatic, dramatic moment. And people kind of sensed that, at that time, this was big. This was big because he was of such high stature already in his career with Philadelphia."

In his first training camp with Green Bay, in the summer of 1993, White assured his new teammate Favre of a different scenario than the one that had played out in punishing fashion the previous fall.

"I told Brett if a guy tries to hit that shoulder again," White announced, "I'll be the first one out on the field for him this year."[4]

When White signed with Green Bay after eight seasons in Philadelphia, he left a familiar world where black enculturation was readily accessible. Suddenly he was in a small town where hardly any blacks lived. Bob Berghaus, sports editor of the *Green Bay Press-Gazette* from 1999 to 2003, comments on the effect that White's presence in nearly all-white Green Bay meant to the franchise's future free agent signees:

"He was the top free agent. A deeply religious man, White said he would go where God wanted him to play," said Berghaus. "Green Bay is the smallest city in the NFL. It's heavily populated by white people. Today, fewer than 2 percent of the population is made up of black people. Back when White—also black—signed, it was less than that.

"Vince Lombardi made black players feel welcome in Green Bay during the 1960s, when the Packers were the toast of the NFL. But the city became less desirable as a place to play for blacks and even for prominent white players when the team struggled in the 1970s and 1980s. White's signing changed all that. Sean Jones, a Pro Bowl defensive end; Keith Jackson, an All-Pro tight end; defensive tackle Santana Dotson; and return specialist Desmond Howard, the most valuable player in the Packers' Super Bowl victory over New England, all signed with the Packers after White came to Green Bay."[5]

~

The bond between coach and players in Green Bay often made for interesting drama. Brett Favre recalled a locker-room meeting the week before the 1995 NFC Divisional Playoff game against San Francisco, head coach Mike Holmgren's hometown and the team with which he was formerly offensive coordinator:

"Mike Holmgren and Reggie White have this deal going," said Favre. "If Mike curses, he gives Reggie's charity a hundred bucks. So, Mike comes into the room, looks around, and the first thing he said was, 'We're going to beat these ——s.' We were shocked. Mike said 'Here' to Reggie and handed him a hundred dollars. Then he looked around and said it even louder. *'We're going to beat these ——s!'* and he forks over another hundred bucks."[6]

Holmgren's spilled emotion and resulting conscientious payment of fines to White launched the Packers to a 27–17 victory over the Niners.

JIM BIEVER PHOTOGRAPHY

White signed a four-year, $17 million contract with the Green Bay Packers on April 8, 1993.

Several of the biggest rivals that White and his Eagle teammates encountered when he was in Philadelphia, in a sense, remained the same after White's switch to Green Bay. This is particularly true of the Cowboys.

If one team consistently had the Packers' number throughout the 1990s, it was Dallas. Green Bay's record against their Texas-sized rival during that decade was a pathetic 1–9, with some of the franchise's biggest heartache losses coming at the hands of the Cowboys, including three straight postseason playoff losses—1993–95—in which the Pack were victims in two Divisional Playoff games and an NFC title game.

Just six days prior to the 1995 NFC Championship Game, White's world had been rocked by news of the firebombing of his all-black Inner City Church in Knoxville, an event that would spawn a host of accusations, conjecture, opposition with investigating agencies, misplaced loyalty, and ultimately, betrayal, as circumstances surrounding the event remain murky and clouded to this day.

With the weight of that catastrophe grinding him down like the heel of a boot on a bug, White began preparing for the biggest game of his life up until that time. Press conferences the week of the game revisited the church burning, giving the premier defensive end little respite from the somberness of the fire's aftermath, further robbing White of precious focus on the huge task at hand in Dallas.

As history records, the Cowboys maintained their mystical domination over Green Bay that day. The humbling 38–27 setback on January 14, 1996, at Texas Stadium, was the most devastating defeat during White's tenure in Green Bay.

Then-*Green Bay Press-Gazette* writer Tony Walter covered that game. "The NFC Championship Game at the end of the '95 season in Dallas was the last game I covered before I moved to South Carolina," says Walter. "I remember being on the field at the end of the game. Dallas won the game by eleven points. I remember afterward, standing kind of at the entrance to where the Packers would go in, and Reggie came storming off the field and was just almost running people over, basically wanting to get away from everybody—almost like he was in a rage. I remember thinking that the disappointment for him at that particular time must have been pretty severe. But I do remember talking to him in the locker room afterwards, and he was in control of himself."

White confessed at the time, "In all my years playing football, from high school to the University of Tennessee to the Memphis Showboats in the United States Football League to the NFL—I had never won a single championship season, not one."

One of pro football's most impressive streaks and mind-boggling oddities is the fact that not once during the fourteen-year Brett Favre era, have the Packers beaten Dallas in Dallas, a formidable 0–8 string that stretches from 1992 through 2004. With the great quarterback's retirement imminent, within a year or two at the most, and with no game scheduled with the Cowboys for 2005, it's all but certain that Favre, barring an unforeseen postseason encounter, will wind up winless in Big D during his entire career.

For White, the Dallas stigma will always be associated with one particular individual, one of the few offensive linemen with the ability to thwart White during his NFL career: Erik Williams, the Cowboys' four-time Pro Bowl tackle. Their titanic matchups rocked the 1990s.

"He's tough to intimidate," White once said of his Dallas nemesis. "He plays furiously, challenges you hard, and keeps coming at you. . . . He quickly gained a rep as one of the few offensive linemen in the league who could make trouble for Reggie White. . . . I enjoy playing against the best, and Erik is still the best offensive tackle in the game."[7]

From Williams's perspective, White was a full day's work, whenever they squared off. "Find me the guy who says Reggie White has lost a step," said Williams in 1993. "Get him down on the field, and I'll make him line up against Reggie so he can see for himself."[8]

One of White's career highlight plays occurred in Dallas on Thanksgiving Day 1994 opposite rookie Larry Allen, later a nine-time Pro Bowl guard for the Cowboys, who was substituting at tackle for the injured Williams. White had sustained a serious elbow injury just four days earlier, against Buffalo, and was not expected to play. Thanks to one of the timely miracles he claims came his way with regard to serious injuries, the Packers' star DE started and played that Thanksgiving Day.

JIM BIEVER PHOTOGRAPHY

White emerges from the tunnel at Lambeau Field.

White opened the proceedings by extending to Allen one of those customary "welcome to the NFL, kid" kind of hellos on the very first play that they lined up against each other. White faked an outside move, which Allen went for, and using only his one good (right) arm, then ripped up and under an off-balanced Allen. Brett Favre describes the rest:

"The most amazing thing I've ever seen Reggie do," said Favre, "was throw the Dallas Cowboys' Larry Allen, a 330-pound offensive lineman, to the turf like he was a rag doll. And that was in the game where Reggie had the elbow injury. He threw him five yards. Just tossed him in the air. I'm standing on the sidelines telling myself, *Jee-zuz Christ! This guy is amazing!*[9]

As much trouble as the Cowboys presented for Green Bay, San Francisco was just the opposite. During the Favre-White

era, the Pack was a glittering 5–1 against the 49ers, including two NFC Divisional Playoff victories and the 23–10 NFC Championship Game win in 1997.

Why so great with one, so poor with the other?

"They were our Goliath," says Sean Jones, White's Green Bay teammate and fellow defensive end, of the Cowboys. "They were a team that just matched up incredibly well against us. It was an interesting scenario. Ironically enough, you're really talking about a 'trinity,' if you will. The trinity was the Green Bay Packers, the San Francisco 49ers, and the Dallas Cowboys. What made it interesting was, Dallas couldn't beat San Francisco, we couldn't beat Dallas, but San Francisco couldn't beat us.

"If you saw how it played out, we beat the pants off San Francisco. Had we gotten Dallas, God knows what would've happened," Jones said, referring to the fact that the Carolina Panthers upset Dallas in the '96 divisional playoffs, and therefore the Packers never had to play their arch nemesis en route to their Super Bowl XXXI victory. "We just could not [beat them]. In every era, there's always that one team. Every team has one [an unbeatable foe]. Indianapolis is going through that now with New England.

"It was just an interesting bit of circumstances [Green Bay-Dallas]. They [the losses] were very demoralizing, because you always felt that you were up for that game. Especially for Reggie, because he had to play against Erik Williams, who just played Reggie extremely well. This guy would just be horrible against other people, but then when it came time to play against Reggie, his style was a style that Reggie didn't play very well against. They were very hard-fought battles that resulted in losses, and I know everyone felt it."

Three major injuries, including the torn ligaments in his elbow mentioned earlier, threatened White's play during a thirteen-month span from October 1994 to December 1995. Jones recalls a game in 1995, a 27–24 loss to Minnesota at the Metrodome, when both he and White seriously collided going after Vikings quarterback Warren Moon from their respective end positions.

"What I remember is that I actually went back in the game and lost a week," says Jones of the play. "I didn't remember anything, and I still don't remember anything that happened two weeks prior to that. Watching the film, I'm thinking, *Wait a second. That game was at home!* Because only two weeks before that, we had played them at home. I don't have any recollection of what I saw on that film."

A somewhat comic moment took place while both players were stretched out on the ground, White with a leg injury that later revealed torn ligaments and Jones semi-conscious from a concussion incurred from the impact of White's knee to his head.

"I remember being laid out on the ground and seeing a crowd of medical staff coming up," says Jones, "and they ran right by me and said, 'Reggie, are you okay?' That was kind of funny, but it was kind of embarrassing when it happened. They were like, 'We know you're okay. You're gonna go back in the game.' I bounced up and didn't know that I was dazed and confused and did go back into the game. It's funny, Reggie and I actually talked about that when we both came around. I used to get on him after that. I'd say, 'You know, you're supposed to go high and *I'm* supposed to go low.'"

Apparently, according to Jones, the incident in Minnesota wasn't the only time he and White failed to communicate on the field. "He always blamed me for the hardest hit he ever took," says Jones. "We were running a game one time, and once again, Reggie didn't always pay attention when we were on the field. You'd tell him to do something, and he was just such a great individual player that he could get away with things most humans couldn't get away with. So, I told him, 'I'm coming around,' and he paid no attention. As soon as I came inside, the tackle was looking right at Reggie and knocked the crap out of him. He said that was the hardest hit he'd taken and it was my fault because I didn't tell him. I said, 'Reggie, I *told* you!'"

Concurring with Jones's assessment of White's rugged "individualism" on the field, fellow defensive line mate and six-year starter Santana Dotson noted that White tended to do his own thing.

"My job, because of where I am in the line, in between the two ends, is to communicate, to call and signal and strengthen up and down the line," remembers Dotson. "I recall a lot of times there would be a certain stunt that we would put on. A stunt is something where everybody has to be on the same page. For instance, Reggie may have to come down inside and I would have to loop around. There were several times, especially my first couple of years there, where something would come in from the sidelines, and Reggie would be like, 'Oh no! I'm not running it. I got it set up. I'm doing my thing!'

"After two or three games of that, I knew automatically when Reggie would get that look on his face. I could look at him and tell: Reggie does *not* want to run a gang, he does *not* need to call, he is locked in and focused! From that, you would get the club move, the 300-pound man hurtling over a running back, jumping and hitting the quarterback in the mouth."

White's remarkable and near-immediate healing from the trio of serious injuries have become part of Reggie White lore. Only four weeks after the Minnesota game, against Cincinnati, the third one occurred: White snapped his hamstring. Media

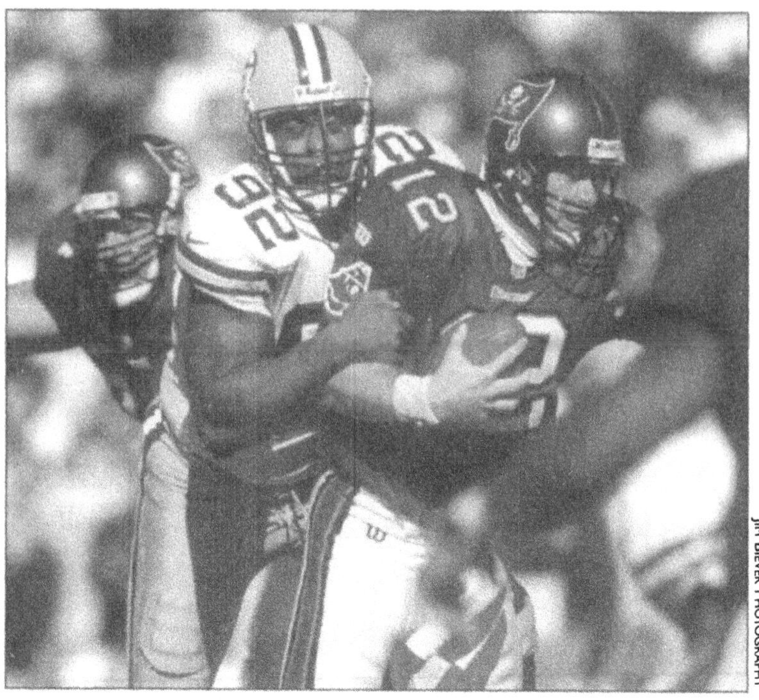

Jim Biever Photography

A ramblin' Reggie collars Tampa Bay quarterback Trent Dilfer.

coverage of the injury generated headlines declaring that the perennial Pro Bowler would be lost for the season. As it turned out, it would be yet another instance of a miraculous recovery in which the star defender was astonishingly healed.

Though not instantaneous, White's third miracle healing came in a time frame clearly qualifying it to be labeled inexplicable. But for the first time in his career, the durable gladiator missed a game (Tampa Bay) due to injury. Initially thinking he could wait out the injury, it became clear that surgery would be necessary to reattach White's balled up, torn hamstring. The procedure was scheduled for the day of the New Orleans game, two weeks after the injury had occurred in Cincinnati.

Prophetically, the week of the Saints game, a Packer teammate's mother had told her son that White would be the recipient of yet another powerful healing.

Indeed, that's exactly what happened. In mid-week—a week and a half after the injury—White, playing with his children at home, felt a sudden strength and mobility return to the leg. Under the supervision of the team's strength coach, Kent Johnston, White underwent a series of sprints and leg-strength tests. The marvel of it all elicited a reaction of utter disbelief from Johnston. White was so overcome by the results, he called on Mike Holmgren at the head coach's home late that Wednesday night to inform him of the astounding turn of events. Only that morning, White had announced to teammates and the press that he was done for the year.

Upon hearing the good-news announcement, Jones revealed to White that he had actually had a dream the night before of his friend standing before him at his locker stall, telling Jones that he would be able to play the following Sunday at New Orleans instead of being on the operating table.

"Absolutely," claims Jones of the prescient experience. "There was no doubt in my mind, because Reggie was a man who lived by his faith. He was a firm believer. Faith and deeds. He did what he had to do and had a strong belief in what could be done, and it happened. Once he told me how he was going to pursue it, there was no doubt in my mind that he was going to be able to play. I didn't say he was going to be healed, but I knew he was going to be able to play."

The occurrence created a stir among the Wisconsin media. Reporters interviewed people on the street, gauging reaction to White's implausible recovery. A few expressed such awe that they considered religious conversion. Jones noted that, while the public may have been amazed and the press somewhat skeptical, Packer teammates were well aware of White's profound relationship with God.

"It was more the media's reaction than teammates' reaction," says Jones. "Reggie had such control of that team spiritually that if he told them that he believed this, then spiritually they believed he could do it. Not absurd things like, 'Okay, I'm about to part water,' nothing like that. Being injured, as long as something's not broken, torn off, or whatever, is a matter of how you manage pain. And someone's going to give you the faith and the belief to manage that pain, and you're going to be able to do that.

"We knew that Reggie was going to be able to do it. Reggie was going to get that strength from someplace, and that's what he did. Some guys don't have the ability to do that, because their helping hand rests at the end of their fingers. Reggie's extended to someplace else. He always had the ability to grasp that helping hand whenever he needed it. No one doubted it."

Brett Favre, in his book *Favre: For the Record*, relates his response to the White hamstring injury and subsequent healing phenomenon. "There are a lot of skeptics out there who wonder whether Reggie's torn hamstring was actually cured by God near the end of the 1995 season," said Favre. "The popular story was the one that said Reggie was lying on the training table when a flash of light zapped his hamstring. Look, I'm not going to argue with the guy. All I know is he was injured and then he was healed. It was a miracle. That's all I can think of.

"A lot of people ask me what really happened. All I can say is Reggie played and there was no way he should have been able to. One hamstring was torn, and he still played at what looked like full speed. Hell, maybe he was only at 75 percent, but I'll take him at 75 percent over anyone else in the league. The miracle thing has happened to him several times. I say whatever works, stay with it. Nothing dramatic like that has happened to me, but if Reggie gets injured again, I'll be the first one praying for another miracle."[10]

Broadcaster Joe Theismann, the former Washington Redskins quarterback, covered the game in which White made his miraculous return from the torn hamstring and even had a rare close inspection of White's injury before the game.

"On the football field, White was a rare combination of size, power, and speed," said Theismann. "He was one of those guys who stepped up and made special plays when his team needed him to come through. Like all great players, he had a great sense of knowing when to seize the moment. I'll never forget, when I was broadcasting the game for *Sunday Night Football*, he'd torn his hamstring, and I remember in the meeting I actually put my fingers in his leg where the hamstring was supposed to be. I expressed shock that he'd be able to play, and he told me he put his faith in God; that it'd be all right. He went out and had a great game, and it was one of the greatest sights I've ever seen. His play that day convinced me of divine intervention. That was typical of the type of faith that Reggie White had. He knew God would take care of the situation."[11]

Santana Dotson, a close friend of White both during and after their playing days together in Green Bay, can still picture his pal's natural fraternal and paternal instincts, traits that often came to light in the locker room.

"It just seems like, in the locker room, he was everybody's big brother and almost father, because a lot of guys came from single-parent backgrounds," says Dotson, who starred at defensive tackle for the Tampa Bay Buccaneers for four seasons before coming to Green Bay. "He never took anything too close to heart. Reggie never took anything too serious about a person, particularly because he's so spiritual. A lot of young guys might think he was unapproachable or hard to come up and talk to, but he was never that way."

Dotson recalls an "almost-incident" one day between White and the late linebacker Wayne Simmons that threatened to rip open the harmony/unity normally associated with the locker room of a contender.

"One time Reggie and a linebacker had a big altercation before a pre-season game, just over playing the radio," remembers Dotson. "The linebacker, Wayne Simmons, wasn't playing at all; he was injured, and he was playing the radio real loud in the locker room. Reggie's statement was, 'Well, why don't you let the people who are getting ready for the game get mentally prepared? Everybody doesn't want to listen to the music." It was a big deal; you physically had to separate the two of them. Simmons stood his ground and Reggie stood his.

"It was my first year then, and I'm, 'Oh my goodness, is there going to be a team meeting about this? Are the coaches going to find out? There's no telling what's going to happen!' I walk into the locker room the next morning and they're both laughing and joking about the *Bugs Bunny* series that was on that morning. That's the type of personality Reggie was: he never took too much to heart. He never had a problem with letting things go when people were human, and everybody had their own human attributes and qualities."

Jones also recalls the infamous locker room episode with Simmons. "It was funny, because Reggie was a gentle giant," says Jones. "Reggie wouldn't fight anybody. Wayne was kind of like the antichrist. They began to mix it up. To see the two of them was like fire and water. But then, ten minutes later, out on the practice field, everything was fine. It was just interesting, the whole dynamics of the thing. There are so many stories involving Reggie. You could write a book on just the stories themselves."

~

Brett Favre remembers White playfully picking on him for being from Mississippi. "He said he wouldn't ever visit me down there because he would be lynched," Favre said. "I know Reggie was just giving me a hard time; Lord knows I tease him enough. I told Reggie that my best friend in high school, Beno Lewis, is black. I know Reggie was just kidding, but I think he was surprised to hear that."[12]

~

Of the many moments Jones prizes from his days in Green Bay, the one experience that he yearns for most is a particular regular gathering with teammates "away from the ball."

"I'll tell you, a lot of guys when they retire miss certain things about football," says Jones. "What I missed the most when I retired was our men's accountability group. I don't know how it got started. There was this bunch of guys that said, 'We need to talk to one another.' Reggie was one of the guys, Keith Jackson, myself, Eugene Robinson, Santana Dotson, Harry Galbreath, Ken Ruettgers. . . . It was a group I really believe in a lot of ways contributed to the success that we had as a team.

"We had a thing called Camaraderie Night on Thursdays, where the guys would go out and eat and have a beer, and Reggie came to that. And you know Reggie doesn't drink. But because of the so-called peer pressure and the precedent that he wanted to instill on that whole situation, he made it clear that he wanted to be a part of it. I think that contributed to the overall success of our football team, because we were not just close on the field, we found ways to be close off the field, and Reggie was a big part of that."

~

Gilbert Brown, the gigantic, 343-pound nose tackle (1993–99, 2001–03) who played side by side with White for six seasons, felt a filial relationship with White and was awed by the superstar's breadth as a person.

"Everything he did, I watched. Everything he did, I tried to do," said Brown, who was claimed off waivers by the Packers in the summer of 1993, the same year White came to Green Bay. "I couldn't do the things he could do, but I looked up at him like I was his son and he was my father."

Brown was asked by Packers beat writer Chris Havel what made White such a great player.

"His stature. His attitude. His power. His knowledge," said Brown. "He was like a book on *How to Play Defensive Line in the NFL*. There was nobody better. Nobody better. I've seen that man throw grown men around the field like they were rag dolls, and he'd be the first one to help them up. That was the guy I knew on the field.

"Off the field, the kindest thing Reggie ever did for me was to tell me how to be a man. Reggie was everything to me. He led by example. He led mentally. He led physically. When we'd get down and tired, we'd look over there and see Reggie still going strong. The words he put together in so many meetings to get us over the hump were amazing."

In Havel's article, Brown said he believed that the Packers' front four of Sean Jones, Santana Dotson, White, and himself might have been one of the best ever. "You got Reggie leading the charge, Sean Jones lining up at the other end, and Santana and me bringing up the rear. That was pretty good," Brown said. "That was a defensive line not to be messed with."[13]

When the future Packers powerhouse of the mid–1990s was in its infancy, in White's first year with Green Bay, in 1993, a

Sunday night home game in October with Denver pitted one of the game's best quarterbacks, John Elway, against one of the game's future best in Favre. It was a classic, going right down to the wire. Tony Walter covered the game that night for the *Green Bay Press-Gazette*:

"I spent the game down on the field," recalls Walter, "I was doing some sort of a different story. John Elway was playing, and Reggie took over the game in the fourth quarter."

The Broncos made a compelling comeback from a 30–7 deficit. With just under two minutes left in the game, Denver, trailing now just 30–27, got the ball back on an interception. That's when White went to work.

"It was a contested game," remembers Walter. "The Packers were up by less than a touchdown, and Elway was known for his great comebacks. Denver got the ball, but on back-to-back plays Reggie got to Elway and sacked him [for eight- and fourteen-yard losses, the last one with 1:27 to go]. The stadium just went nuts. I remember thinking specifically, *Wow, he really is taking over the game!* Reggie was basically just saying, 'No, this isn't going to happen.' Reggie in the fourth quarter—oooh! He was just dominant."

Afterward, White gave a compelling quote regarding the game's final two minutes, in particular the drive-halting plays on Elway. "Somebody had to make the play, and somebody did."[14]

The victory turned around the 1–3 Packers, who then won seven of their next eleven games to reach the playoffs for the first time since 1982.

Walter also recalls White's homecoming in Philadelphia two years after leaving the Eagles via his landmark free agency case, when he signed with Green Bay. It was a mid-September

1994 game at Veterans Stadium, and the Packers went down, 13–7. Eleven years later, Walter revisits a memory from that game completely inconsequential to the final score.

"The Eagles won when the Packers failed on fourth down, right down on the 5-yard line at the end of the game," recounts Walter. "I remember Reggie and Eric Allen, the Eagles cornerback and a very good friend of Reggie's, getting together afterward. Allen had come into the Packer locker room after he had already changed and dressed. He and Reggie just had a real poignant moment, because this was their first time opposing each other [in Philadelphia]. I remember getting a sense of how difficult it must have been for Reggie to make the move [to Green Bay]."

~

With White on board, Packer team meetings were seldom dull. According to Brett Favre: "Every week when Mike [Holmgren] goes to give out the Defensive Player of the Week award, everybody chants, "Reg-GIE! Reg-GIE!' We're pretty sure Mike and Reggie are related. Mike will be like, 'Okay, settle down. This week's defensive award goes to . . . Reggie White.' And everybody will start laughing. Then Mike will say, 'No, just joking. It goes to Doug Evans' or whatever. It's a pretty lively session."[15]

~

Santana Dotson reflects on the difference playing for a habitual doormat like the Tampa Bay teams from the Bucs' first twenty-year era, as opposed to the salad days with Green Bay:

"The biggest thing coming from Tampa to Green Bay," says Dotson, "was getting an opportunity to play with a great man and defensive lineman like Reggie White, and also Sean Jones, and Gilbert Brown, who was coming up as well. Everybody remembers my great days at Green Bay, and I was a great individual talent in Tampa Bay, but it never prospered, and that kind of shows you how much of a team sport football really is. I was very excited about going up to play with the likes of Reggie and Sean and Gilbert.

"I don't remember many football conversations with Reggie, though. He was the type of guy that was always asking about your family, how you were doing off the field, how you were as a man, your faith. He was never pushing or forcing anything on you, but he sincerely cared about your walk."

Another former Tampa Bay Buccaneer, linebacker Hardy Nickerson, says some of the Bucs' offensive tackles were a little less than enthusiastic about taking on the physical White mano a mano.

"Yeah, I joked with them," laughs Nickerson. "Anytime we played the Packers, it was like, 'Okay, Jerry Wunsch, it's your turn this week!' Yeah, Paul Gruber and those guys, they were quite nervous leading up to a game with the Packers."

White's passing was the latest in a series of deaths befalling members of 1990s Packer teams. The string of human losses, starting in 1999, began with the death of the club's defensive coordinator, Fritz Shurmur, who died at age sixty-seven of esophageal and liver cancer in August of that year. Shurmur was scheduled to join Mike Holmgren's staff in Seattle when the former Packers head coach headed west to begin the 1999 season, but the esteemed defensive mentor passed away before the season started.

Linebacker Wayne Simmons, mentioned earlier for his involvement in a volatile locker room shouting match with

White, died in a single-vehicle crash in August 2002 in Independence, Missouri, after his car went off the road as a result of reckless driving at high speeds. Simmons, with the Packers from 1993 to 1997 and a starter during the '96 Super Bowl championship season, had been traded by Green Bay to Kansas City just eight months after the team's victory in Super Bowl XXXI. After spending a year and a half in K.C. and half of the 1998 season with Buffalo, Simmons was gone from the league.

Though not a part of the Packers' family, White of course also lost Eagles teammate Jerome Brown in 1992.

The ultimate moment in White's professional football career, the one thing he pined, prayed, and pointed for, finally came to pass on January 26, 1997, in the Louisiana Superdome. After falling short of their goal the previous three seasons in the playoffs, including a tough loss in the 1995 NFC Championship Game to Dallas, the Packers were finally headed to the Super Bowl.

Before the big game against the AFC's New England Patriots for the world title, tension was at a peak in the Green Bay locker room.

Quarterback Brett Favre, who admitted that his own heart was pounding out of his chest, looked over at White.

"Reggie was getting really emotional on us," said Favre. "He had this look of determination and pride and intensity that I'd never seen before. It was an awesome sight."[16]

White, of course, had made it plain to everyone in the Western world that a Super Bowl ring was his unwavering goal. It had been part of his disillusionment with the Eagles' brass when he was in Philadelphia, when he determined over the span of his eight seasons there that Norman Braman's

Jim Biever Photography

White and Brett Favre, above, share a moment during the trophy presentation following Super Bowl XXXI, January 26, 1997, in New Orleans, where the Packers defeated New England, 35–21. That's Fox Sports' Terry Bradshaw interviewing Packer head coach Mike Holmgren at right. On the flight back home after the Packers' win in Super Bowl XXXI, Reggie shows just how he feels about the coveted Vince Lombardi Trophy.

crew was not truly committed to the idea of winning championships, and White had made it abundantly clear when visiting teams on the "Reggie Tour" that he was looking for the kind of dedicated management from a team that spelled Super Bowl. At last, the goal, the right team, and he were collectively on the brink of his longtime dream.

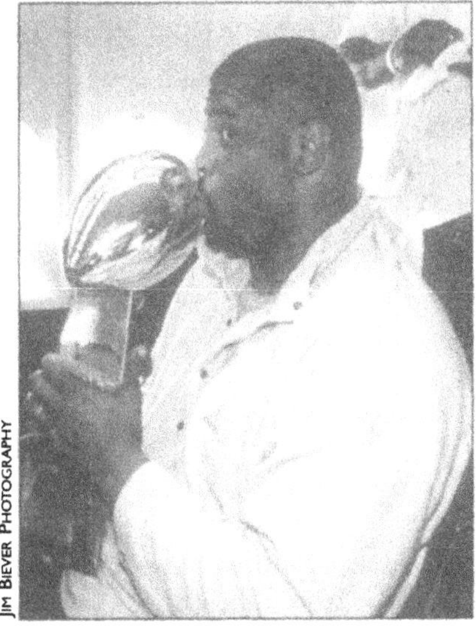

Jim Biever Photography

JIM BIEVER PHOTOGRAPHY

The Super Bowl XXXI champion Packers visit with President Bill Clinton at the White House in May 1997.

The Pack took an early 10–0 lead, when Favre audibled on Green Bay's second play from scrimmage, hitting wide receiver Andre Rison on a forty-four-yard post pattern for the game's first touchdown. On the ensuing drive by New England, linebacker Doug Evans's interception of a Drew Bledsoe pass led to a thirty-seven-yard Chris Jacke field goal and a quick ten-point lead.

But the Patriots retaliated behind two Bledsoe scoring aerials to take a 14–10 advantage at the conclusion of the frenetic first quarter, the highest-scoring opening period in Super Bowl history.

The second quarter was dominated by Green Bay, as Favre connected with wide receiver Antonio Freeman on the longest scoring pass in Super Bowl history, an eighty-one-yarder. Favre then scored himself on a two-yard bootleg. The reliable Jacke added three more points.

New England whittled the score to within a touchdown before Packers return man Desmond Howard ran back the ensuing kickoff ninety-nine yards, the longest scoring play in Super Bowl history, for the back-breaker that sewed up the game for Green Bay. Howard also registered key punt-return runbacks of thirty-two and thirty-four yards to become the first special teams player in Super Bowl history (just how many records did these guys set?) to be awarded the game's MVP trophy.

White set yet one more Super Bowl record—for most sacks, with three—critically bringing down Bledsoe on back-to-back sacks during the Pats' drive that immediately followed Howard's wrap-it-up kickoff return.

"Everyone in the place knew Reggie was going to put heat on Drew Bledsoe," said Favre, "but the Patriots decided to block him one on one anyway. Bad move. Reggie iced the game with a Super Bowl record three sacks down the stretch. When he racked up his last one, in the fourth quarter, I stepped into the huddle and said, 'Well, men. We're Super Bowl champs.'"

JIM BIEVER PHOTOGRAPHY

Against San Francisco in the Packers' 23–10 NFC Championship Game victory at 3Com Park on January 11, 1998, White notched three tackles and a sack.

White's performance in New Orleans that afternoon gave Favre pause for reflection on his teammate's superlative and far-from-diminishing skills.

"You see him getting blocked by two and three people, and you laugh when fans wonder why his sack totals are down," said Favre. "Look at it. When he's single-blocked, he beats people. In the Super Bowl, the Patriots decided to let Max Lane try to block him one on one. He embarrassed the kid. You just can't do that with Reggie. You can't go into a game thinking Reggie is hurting and he's getting older, so you don't double him. That kind of thinking gets quarterbacks killed. Reggie can still dominate like no other player in the league. Period."[17]

Pinnacle attained. Dream fulfilled. White will be forever remembered for his jog around the perimeter of the massive Superdome's interior, Vince Lombardi Trophy in hand.

"With my heart in my throat and tears in my eyes, I grabbed the Lombardi Trophy and ran around the field, holding it high," said White of his career moment. "I understand there were three Cheeseheads for every Patriots fan in the Superdome that day. . . . I wanted those fans and all the people back home to know: this trophy belongs to you as much as us!"[18]

"This trophy . . . this is it. It was named after Vince Lombardi. You play in Green Bay. As important as it is to any other team and any other player, it means more to *us*."

— Mike Holmgren

Jan. 26, 1997, to his Super Bowl XXXI champion Green Bay Packers in the locker room following the game, twenty-nine years after the franchise's last world championship.

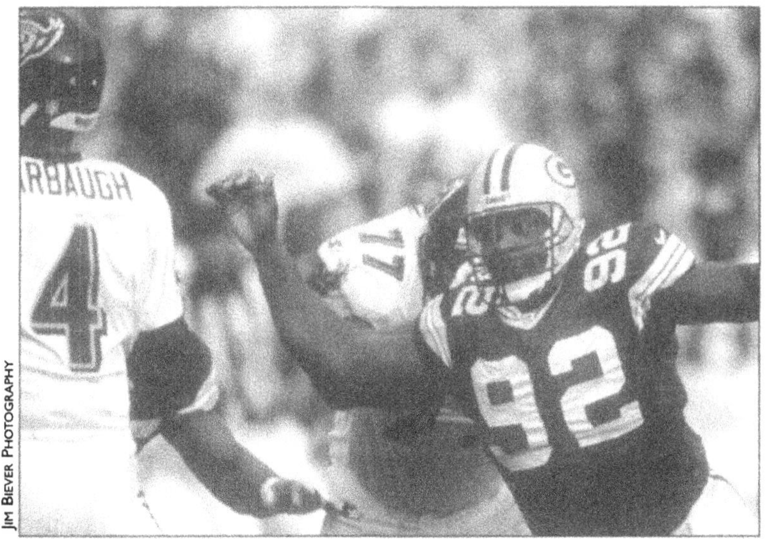

JIM BIEVER PHOTOGRAPHY

White bears down on Ravens quarterback Jim Harbaugh during the Packers' 28–10 victory on October 25, 1998.

"Last time Green Bay won a title, I was five years old—
Brett Favre hadn't even been born yet!"
— Reggie White

"For God so loved the Packers He sent them Reggie."
— Sign outside First United Church of Christ
in Green Bay, the morning of Super Bowl XXXI.

7

The Minister

In sports, it is the rule rather than the exception that an athlete's particular sport is his or her life. And an all-consuming life it is, demanding a level of dedication and commitment that leaves little time for anything else. Too often that means little quality time with families and missed opportunities for personal growth.

To the friends and teammates of Reggie White, it was mind-boggling enough to observe the uncanny power, speed, and technique that made him one of the most complete and awe-inspiring athletes ever to take the field, as witnessed by the *Sporting News*' selection of White as the twenty-second-greatest football player of all time in 1999. But paramount play on the gridiron was only one element of the man they called the Minister of Defense. The "Minister" side of White, significantly, would carry far more weight in his life, his godly presence and rock-solid faith birthing a formidable leader and champion of human rights.

White always credited his introduction to Christianity to his grandmother, Mildred Dodds, who took him and his younger brother, Julius, under her care for a year when Reggie was seven, as mentioned earlier in Chapter Two. "Miss Mildred" never forced religion on the boys, but rather made it seem more like a privilege to visit God's sanctuary, which occasioned a five-mile walk each way on Sundays and Wednesday evenings.

White also credits the white pastor of that all-black church as a major influence in turning over his life to Christ. In his autobiography, *In the Trenches*, White asserts that the Reverend Bernard Ferguson "was one of the most sincere, authentic examples of true Christianity I've ever known—a totally selfless man who genuinely cared for people."[1]

By the time Reggie entered high school, he had already been saved. But the dichotomy of athlete and religious devotee proved a confusing combination for some of White's classmates at Chattanooga's Howard High School. White did not fit the classic mold of the prototypical jock.

"They made fun of him, you know, in high school, when he carried his Bible with him," says Herman Prater Sr. of Chattanooga, a longtime friend of the White family who had photographed White since the ninth grade. "Being a football player, it was kind of strange to see someone like that walking around with a Bible. He believed in the Word."

White's basketball coach at Howard, Henry Bowles, who guided the Hustlin' Tigers for twenty-nine years as well as serving as an assistant coach in football, also taught White in a psychology/sociology class. With a chuckle, Bowles recalls a tale involving White's already strong connection to Bible study conflicting with his regular classroom work.

"When he came to us he definitely had his Bible with him on a daily basis," says Bowles, recently honored with the naming of the Henry Wesley Bowles Gymnasium at Howard. "He was reading his Bible in class one time, when we were preparing for an examination. I said, 'Reggie? That Bible will get you to heaven, but you got to pass this test to get you out of here. You find in that Bible where it tells you there is a time for everything under the sun. And this is *not* the time to read the Bible.'

"Reggie's first cousin was in the class, and she was a very good student. He said, 'Vanessa's taking notes. I'm gonna look at her notes.' With Reggie, he always exemplified a good religious and spiritual background, and I feel his grandmother was responsible for that."

Of course, White was well known for bringing his religious convictions onto the field of play as well. From the high school ranks through the pros, his ministry was a continuous work in progress, and countless occasions would arise for the Minister of Defense to minister those beliefs.

"Another time, we were in a state tournament in Murfreesboro," Bowles continues. "It was always my procedure to pray before and after a ball game—win, lose, or draw. I would always invite the kids to pray. If they didn't care, they could just pull away to the other side of the room. We'd already had our prayer and it was now halftime; we weren't doing too well. We got ready to leave the locker room, having gone over some adjustments we thought might help us. Before we started out, Reggie hollered, 'Coach! Can we pray?' I said, 'Reggie, we've already prayed. The Lord is waiting for us to do some of the things that *we* promised Him. He's keeping His promise. We're all breathing; we're alive.'

"After I got through with this sermon, Reggie said, 'Coach, I still want to pray.' I said, 'Okay, Reggie, you win.' He was just that type of person. If he had a conviction, he was going to stick to it. I was impressed with that, even through I was a little peeved at the time."

White's football coach at Howard, Robert Pulliam, witnessed many instances of the young Reggie relative to his budding ministerial work and intense devotion to religious study.

"I remember when I visited with him, when he was in junior high, and he shared with me his feelings about the Word and what he wanted to do in life, which was to be a minister," recalls Pulliam, now principal of Henderson Independent High School, an alternative school in Salisbury, North Carolina. "Well, I ended up having a team meeting—I was primarily talking to my seniors—and told them about this young person who was going to come and be a part of our program. I asked each and every one of them if they would vow to join me in doing everything that we could do to support his direction.

"Howard High School at the time was very at-risk; it had lots of problems. I wanted to solicit our players' support to stand by him and not allow anyone to . . . you know how kids can be. I also knew that Reggie was a Bible-toter throughout middle school. Coming into high school, there was no doubt about it: you would not catch him on that campus without the Bible in his hand.

"I never will forget, after talking to the team and seeing signs that everybody received Reggie well, there was a situation with Reggie in study hall, in his first year," Pulliam continues. "One of my captains, one of my seniors, happened to be in that class with him. He and Reggie had come to see me one day, and I didn't really know what it was about, until they started sharing the story.

"For every other kid in the class, study hall was fun time. Everybody's going to get together to talk and play. This fellow, the senior captain, told me he noticed the first day that he went in there that Reggie was sitting upfront by himself. Everybody else was in little groups, cutting up, having a good time. Ol' Reggie was sitting up there reading something. A couple girls, couple guys walked by, saw what he was reading, and went back and reported it to their group. They started getting ready to taunt.

"Ol' Roland, the captain, told me, 'Coach, in an instant I remembered what you said.' Being the football captain and a senior, he was pretty hardcore, getting a lot of respect from his peers. So what he decided to do, remembering what we had vowed and knowing that the other kids weren't going to taunt if he was in the mix, he went up and sat with Reggie.

"He said, 'Coach, the first day, I just faked them out. I didn't read a word. Made them think I was looking.' So they left it alone. The second day Roland said, 'Coach, I saw them getting ready [to taunt Reggie], so I went back up there again. This time I read about a paragraph with him.' On the third day, the kids in the class were getting ready to start the same movement. Roland told me, 'Coach, I sat there and I read an entire chapter with him. And it was *good!*'"

The two then approached Pulliam to get his take on a matter of importance to them that just happened to fly in the face of a federal edict.

"Back in my days as a young football coach, they had taken prayer out of the schools," remembers Pulliam. "I wasn't real smart, but I knew enough that I couldn't insist on making folks pray. So, I disguised it. With the football team, before a game, we'd get together, hold hands, and have a moment of silence. But I didn't fool anybody; the kids knew exactly what we were doing.

"Now, Roland and Reggie came to me. Reggie wasn't yet a spokesman. Roland was a spokesman. He began to tell me that he and Reggie had had a discussion. They said, 'Coach, looking back on this fall, we are mighty afraid. Many of our teammates, the only time they pray in the course of a week or even during a year is during football time on Friday nights. We feel that it's essential that people pray more.'

"So, they asked me, 'Coach, can we—spring, fall, anytime this football team gets together—can we have a moment of prayer?'

"'You said it; let's do it,' I said."

White's high school teammates and coaches paid him a high compliment when many showed up for his first sermon and subsequent ordination as a Baptist minister at age seventeen.

"He invited us for his first sermon," remembers Bowles. "This was at his grandmother's church. I think, out of fifteen guys, we had about eight people with him there that Sunday morning. They respected him. They respected his beliefs. They knew he was serious."

Pulliam was also there, along with a recruiter from the University of Tennessee named Bobby Jackson.

"I remember sitting with Bobby when Reggie reached his trial sermon in high school," says Pulliam. "Bobby kind of took his elbow and poked me in the side and said, 'Coach, just look at him. Who in the world wouldn't listen to somebody who looked like that? He'd tell you to believe!'

"Reggie had a way of cultivating other folks. I constantly read and read the Bible, but I never preached to nobody. I tried to be an example. I knew what God had entrusted in me from the moment that I had that first visit with Reggie. The thing I really loved about him, he would read that Bible. You'd see it with him everywhere, but he would never stop and try to preach to you. I'd never known him to do that."

When White arrived in Knoxville to begin his four-year play at the University of Tennessee under head coach Johnny Majors, he naturally brought his belief system with him. Friendships were formed with other student-athletes, and their likenesses and similarities were soon revealed. It wasn't long before an aggregate of Christians found one another on the squad and began assembling for prayer.

"Reggie, Willie Gault, and Anthony Hancock went to church regularly—we had a lot of players that went to church regularly—and they would come into the Sunday training table, several of them with their Bibles in their hands," remembers Majors. "They'd just been to church and had their best coat and shirt and tie on. Reggie and Willie would come in to see me a couple of times a year, wanting me to testify on my TV show I had every Sunday morning.

"Reggie would say, 'I think you ought to testify on TV, Coach. That would be good for everybody. We also want to put "appear for prayer" on the practice schedule.'

"I said, 'Fellas, I heard my grandmother Majors testify in church, and she believed everything she said. She was a fine, religious woman. But that's not my style, and it wasn't my dad's style or my mother's style. But I go to church, and I try to do things decently. I can't say that I always do, and I'm not trying to tell you that I'm an altar boy, but I'm not gonna put prayer on the practice schedule. I wouldn't feel comfortable, and it would be hypocritical if I did.

"'We have people who maybe don't believe the way you guys believe, or they may be people of a different religion. There are not many Muslims or Jewish kids playing, but if there are people out there, I don't care whether they're Hindu or Buddhist, I'm gonna coach them, too, and we're not gonna force prayer on anybody. But if you want to get there early before practice starts, or if you want to stay after practice, you can pray all you want to on the football field. I'm not gonna do that, but I respect your feelings.' That event showed that Reggie had a lot confidence, and I was very respectful of that."

Majors, an All-America triple-threat tailback for the Tennessee Volunteers in 1956 who finished second in the Heisman Trophy balloting to Paul Hornung that same year, guided the University of Pittsburgh to a national championship in 1976 before returning to his alma mater the following year, where he would post a 116–62–8 record during his 16 years as head coach of the Big Orange. He continues about White's beliefs:

"I think some people can distance themselves from others with their personal and religious views," says Majors, "but Reggie's were so sincere, and he was so likable and lovable as a teammate and so aggressive and so productive as a player that people didn't question him at all. Not that he was going to threaten to whip them. He had such a dominating physical physique and such a dominating personality that people believed what he was saying and Reggie believed what he was saying. When he would say that God spoke to him, Reggie believed that. And if that was his belief, who am I to question it?

"What Reggie did say, he said with verve and vitality and sincerity. He was believable in the way that he said it, and you knew that he was sincere. He didn't come on as an Elmer Gantry-type preacher."

UT teammate, friend, and roommate Willie Gault, a tremendously gifted athlete who not only starred as an All-America wide receiver and punt/kick returner for the Vols (1982) but also was at one time ranked No. 2 in the world in the 110-meter high hurdles and qualified for the 1980 U.S. Olympic

Team in three events, shared the love of God and the Bible with White. He agrees with his former collegiate head coach, Majors, on White's presentation as a preacher.

"He would try to tell you the truth, but Reggie had fun also," recalls Gault. "He wasn't a minister in the sense that you'd think of him as this tight-collared guy. He was a guy who loved people. He loved to have fun and enjoyed what he was doing. His religious beliefs didn't distance anyone from him, because Reggie was very committed. People knew that. He was such a nice guy that he would not only tell you what he thought, but he would help you in any way that he could. He enjoyed sports and he loved all types of people. He actually just tried to speak the truth as he knew it at the time.

"People knew that what he said was coming from a guy who loved them, so no one was offended and everyone kind of listened. We were all in the same boat as peers, so it was important that we understand and learn from each other. We learned from some of the guys who weren't Christians, some of the guys who came from different parts of the country, different parts of the world. He learned from us as we learned from him. That was the unique thing about it."

Larry Marmie, defensive coordinator during White's senior season at Tennessee, acknowledges that a special connection existed between him and his prodigious defensive tackle-end in the one season they were together.

In his autobiography, White mentions the immediate respect generated for Marmie because of the assistant coach's unconventional approach to teaching.

"He was a great motivator," said White. "Unlike many coaches who threaten or cuss their players to get them going, Coach Marmie inspired our best efforts through positive motivation. He would much rather draw out our best performance by making us believe in ourselves than by shaming us into action. All of us on the defensive line just loved him, and we were ready to go to war for him."[2]

Marmie, now the defensive coordinator under head coach Mike Martz with the NFL's St. Louis Rams, was impressed with the young man growing before him, a man of strength, purpose, and conviction.

"Reggie would say what was on his mind," says Marmie. "I don't recall a single situation where a person might soft-play something or say 'this is not the right time.' The players and the people who were around him on a daily basis had such great respect for him as a person. The way he handled [his religious beliefs], it was never a circumstance where there was any division. In other words, even guys that didn't share the same personal beliefs that Reggie did had such great respect for him both as a person and a player that they were willing to listen when he spoke. It was much, much more positive the way he handled it. I don't know of any negativity that came about because of Reggie's beliefs."

~

Raleigh McKenzie, a three-year teammate of White at Tennessee and sixteen-year NFL veteran, observed White's Christian influence on more than one occasion on the UT campus.

"It probably put a little bit of a wedge or distance with some people," recalls McKenzie, who recently received his master's in education at age forty-two, "but with Reggie, I think it really brought a lot of people to him. Probably the only kind of wedge going on was from people taking potshots, trying to get him to do different things. 'Hey Reggie, we're going to a party, want to go?' Knowing Reggie, they'd try to get him riled up and say 'All right, now. Don't be out there messin' around.'

Even with the older guys, early on, he was almost like a big brother, and definitely later on, more like a father figure. He did things the right way."

~o~

Current University of Tennessee head coach Phillip Fulmer, a three-year lettering lineman from 1969 to 1971 with the Vols and an offensive line coach under Johnny Majors during White's tenure at UT, recognizes the unique and even historic value of White's religious significance while on The Hill in Knoxville.

"It started even as a freshman," says Fulmer of White's composure and dedication. "When he first came here he was very confident. He obviously had a lot to learn about playing the game, but he was always a very confident person. I know that very early in his freshman year he asked the coaches if he could do the prayer after practice. We still do it, all these years later, because of Reggie doing it.

"Obviously, there were probably a few that might have been uncomfortable with that, but for the most part, everybody accepted Reggie for exactly what he was—a very devout, dedicated, Christian man who was trying to live the life he thought the Lord wanted him to live, and he wanted everyone else to live it with him. He was not one bit embarrassed about talking about that at all."

~o~

Another teammate and onetime roommate of White at Tennessee, Lee Jenkins, an ordained minister in Atlanta, illustrates Fulmer's point about White's commanding presence, even while a collegian.

"We never practiced—like had a real hitting practice—on a Sunday workout," remembers Jenkins. "But this one particular week we must have played bad or something, I don't know, but Johnny Majors made us dress out on a Sunday—pads and everything. Reggie and others were upset, especially the guys like me and him who went to church on Sunday.

"So, Reggie told Coach Majors and the whole coaching staff once we got on the field: 'I just got one thing to say. Since y'all got us out here on a Sunday, you gotta promise there'll be no profanity, no cussing, because this is God's day.' And that's hard for a college coach, not using profanity. I mean just a little bit. So all these coaches were like, 'Oh man, that's going to be tough. A two-hour practice.' But they did it.

"Reggie knew how to talk to people about sensitive religious issues without offending them. I don't know if he ever offended hardly anybody. He definitely inspired people."

After graduating from the University of Tennessee, White elected to launch his professional football career within the state, signing with the United States Football League franchise in Memphis. While there, he met a true friend and brother in Calvin Clark, a fellow defensive end with the Memphis Showboats, who became an ordained minister himself.

"Wherever we traveled on the road, we'd room together," recalls Clark, now heading up his own Front Line Ministry, serving youth, in Denton, Texas. "I remember, before we actually got to know one another, there was a Bible study called by Alan Duncan, the former kicker who had played with Reggie in college at Tennessee. Alan was a young minister also, a missionary who grew up with a missionary family. He actually initiated us getting together as a team to have Bible studies.

"Both Reggie and I showed up. Reggie said, 'Cal! I knew it! I knew you were a Christian! I knew it! I knew there was something about you!' He got so excited, because he really didn't know anybody then. He had nobody, especially on the defensive line, who was a Christian that he could bond with, so he was just so happy to have another defensive lineman as a brother in the Lord. Then we began to room together and had some great, great times.

"I really did consider him like a little brother. I was the captain of the team, and they kind of looked up to me as the elder statesman. But none of them knew that I was only about two or three years older than them. They thought I was older because I was bald. [laughing] They looked at me as an old dude.

"In Reggie's younger days, there was such a natural innocence about him, he was so full of joy," Clark continues. "But then the cameras and all the media kind of whittled away at him and in time took away his joy. Out of all the years that I've known him, he only got upset over two things: 1) the misuse by the media, and 2) the misuse of his friendship by other so-called friends."

Showboats defensive line coach Chuck Dickerson, White's position mentor in Memphis, felt that, in general, his young charge's religious fervor didn't particularly attract or alienate other members of the team.

"I'm not sure that it did either," says Dickerson, now working part-time for ESPN Florida. "I think everybody accepted Reggie's feelings, and those that had the bent followed him and became very close to him, and those that did not feel that open and overt about their inner feelings were a little less in the mainstream. I don't think it affected [his relationship with team members] an awful lot one way or the other.

"It's like anything else: Those that do, do. Those that don't, don't. He never held it against anybody if they weren't religious, because he never held it against me. [laughing] But he certainly made himself available to anybody who needed help or wanted to be close to him in those fashions."

~

White's head coach with the Memphis Showboats, Pepper Rodgers, the team's innovative strategist and *raconteur suprême*, recalls a story with a message involving White's urgent need to bring, as he had done at Tennessee, a sense of religious community and fellowship to team members, under the auspices of the club. Rodgers firmly set the line of division, so there would be no future misunderstandings between them.

"I remember one time we were playing somebody, and Reggie was on the sideline," recounts Rodgers. "You know that he was a very religious person and very vocal about his religious beliefs. Well, he was not playing very well, and I overheard him saying to one of the players or coaches, 'Pray for me to play better.' And I said to him, 'Now, Reggie, listen to me very carefully. If praying were the secret to athletic success, the Russians and the East Germans would never have won a gold medal. And, Reggie, they're atheists!' I said, 'Now, if you want to get to heaven, pray for it. But if you want to start playing better, get your ass in gear. God gave you that body; you're six foot five, 290 pounds, and run like a deer. What more do you want?'"

Continuing, Rodgers waxes philosophical on the subject of religion on the playing field: "Football has always been made up of very religious people. It's the most religious sport out there. Now, don't ask me why. When someone said at the end of practice—it probably was Reggie—'We're going to have a fellowship meeting of Christian athletes after practice.' I said, 'Ex*cuse* me? We don't make speeches at practice except about football. If you want to get everybody after practice and tell them there's a meeting of the ACLU, that there's a meeting of the Jewish Defense Society or the Christian Coalition, fine! But that's not what we do out here.'

"I'm not a man of the cloth; I'm a man of the turf. And while we're on the football field, my thing has always been 'take it off the field.' I don't care what you do [privately], but it's not my job to promote religion. I'm very uncomfortable with trying to do that.

"If you knew me," says Rodgers, "you'd basically know that I have good thoughts, I'm an 'up' guy. If that says that I'm a good Christian, fine. I could be a good Jewish guy; I could be a good whatever! That's why Reggie and I liked one another. He knew who I was, and I liked Reggie. We were friends. He knew his position and I knew my mine. My position was that I was the head coach. His was that he was the best defensive pass rusher in the history of the National Football League."

Philadelphia Eagles wide receiver Mike Quick, who now owns a distribution business in addition to his work as an analyst for Eagles radio broadcasts as well as on television for Comcast, discovered that the locker room is a strangely brewing melting pot—an environment where many things of diverse natures are shared. White's strong profession of faith, he says, was never a problem in the Philly locker room.

"There are some people in a locker room-type setting that, if you shared a personal or religious belief, it would start to turn guys off," says Quick. "They wouldn't want to listen to you. I don't think that ever was an issue in our locker room. It wasn't like Reggie was forcing anything on anybody. But he believed what he believed in, and he stood up for what he believed in. If you had a different approach to life, although he was going to tell you what he felt was right, he respected people that had other ways of living their life.

"A prime example is Jerome Brown. Jerome was in our locker room, and he was a wild, crazy guy who liked to party and liked the fast life, the women, and all. And he and Reggie were probably the best of friends."

Quick has carried an unusual emotional burden along with his other teammates in Philadelphia: losing two team members early to death. Brown was killed in a car crash, along with his twelve-year-old nephew, at age twenty-seven. He was a two-time All-Pro and Pro Bowler in his five brief seasons in the NFL, all with the Eagles. At his funeral, White was asked to speak at the request of Brown's parents. "Every time a life ends," White proclaimed, "there's a purpose. If we don't grab onto that purpose, we lose the whole plan."[3]

"Two great people," Quick adds about his former teammates. "I think one of the things that threw Reggie and Jerome together was that they were very similar. And they both really loved people. Jerome loved to have fun and act crazy, but he really cared about the people around him. A guy like Jerome would do anything for you—give you the shirt off his back. That was just the kind of guy that he was. I think that's why the two of them connected so well. They lived their lives completely different, but down deep both of those men were very similar."

Another teammate of White at Philadelphia, Mike Golic, a defensive tackle from 1987 through 1992, cites the togetherness of the Eagle defenders and still recalls the shock of Brown's loss.

"Our whole D-line had a really good relationship," says Golic. "It's just unbelievable that between the five of us—Mike Pitts, Clyde Simmons, Jerome, Reggie, and me—two of them are dead. It's just an awful thought. I remember them both, obviously too vividly, being called.

"There's no more acceptable way [to die] above the other, I guess, but with Jerome's being an accident—Jerome had the reputation of driving fast; he was a free spirit. In the back of their minds, people never wanted to talk about it, but they always knew that he drove fast and that he could be a reckless guy. You always hoped that nothing would happen. Once you get over the initial shock of him dying in a car accident, the more you think about it, it wasn't as shocking. It's never, obviously, *not* shocking, but you saw it. It was an accident.

"With Reggie, the thing that's tough with him, or even with a guy like Sam Mills [12-year linebacker with New Orleans and Carolina], who just passed away, is that when we play the sport we play for a living—any pro sport, but football especially, because it's so physically demanding—there's obviously a lot of contact. It's kind of a gladiator sport. There's the feeling of invincibility. No one can do anything to you. You're untouchable. You can't be hurt. That's just the mentality you have to have. And if you are hurt, you still have to go play. It's just a warrior mentality.

"And to have a guy like Reggie, the player that he was, the athlete that he was, basically die in his sleep, or from a condition that affected his sleep, and then he's gone; it's just unfathomable to me. It wasn't a car accident; it wasn't a freak thing that would make you just as sad. It's like, how could *this* guy's body give out on him? That's the part that just doesn't ring.

"It's just not in the rightful order of things," Golic states. "For anybody at that age to pass in their sleep, somebody who is known for their body, for their physicality, for the abilities that God gave them with their body, and then just have it give out at forty-three years of age—it just doesn't seem right."

Golic also concurs with Quick that White was never one to attempt turning the Eagles locker room into a fire-and-brimstone evangelism tent.

"There are those that, when they get 'saved,' become kind of pushers of that in a locker room or on their pedestal, when they didn't live in a good way, and then all of a sudden they [get religion], and they feel every body should, and if you don't, you're wrong," says Golic. "That's how some were who got 'saved.' It can become sort of a turnoff. But it was never like that with Reggie.

"Reggie was always sincere in his convictions, and again, never pushed it on anybody. He was always willing to talk about it, but he was very genuine in it, and I appreciated that."

If you've ever wondered what a typical guest appearance by White at a charity, benefit, educational, or church event would be like, this will give you a feel: About 1994 the *Green Bay Press-Gazette*'s Tony Walter, then among staffers covering the Packers, conducted a weekend program on "serving your community," for middle schoolers and high schoolers within the De Pere, Wisconsin, Episcopal diocese, held at St. Anne's Episcopal Church. The visit came on a weekend when the Packers had a bye, and so White was able to attend.

"This was arranged with Sara, his wife," says Walter, now assistant metro editor for the *Press-Gazette*. "I had done an interview with her a couple months before that. She and I met at a pancake restaurant and were talking, and our conversation just kind of went over to what at that time was an avocation of mine, working with the youth of the church, knowing they were heavily involved with church activities. So I just kind of loosely said, 'Gee, would Reggie come and talk to us?' And Sara shot right back, 'Just tell me when.' I'm thinking, Whoa! but then I said, 'But Sara, I don't have the kind of money . . . I can't pay him.' I figured the honorarium he might command would be prohibitive. But she said, 'Don't worry.'

"She basically was the person I communicated with. I would see Reggie occasionally in the work environment—in the locker room or after games, after practice, things like that. But that was different. I wanted to make sure we kept things separate, and he respected that as well.

"Basically, we were talking to the kids about what they could do within their own community," Walter continues. "And Reggie was so effective, because here was somebody taking the gifts and talent that he had and doing things within his own community.

"We had the kids all on the floor. Then Reggie came in, dressed to the nines, because he and his family were going from our church to his church afterward. When he walked in, he was just, of course, a massive individual. He talked to the kids about making a difference in the world where they are. He talked about the fact that he had been given a gift, but also, with that gift there was a responsibility and that he needed to use it, that just playing football wasn't enough.

"Reggie talked to them for about twenty minutes, just basically challenging them: 'You're probably not going to be a football player, but you can make just as big of an impact as I can.' It resonated with them. It was certainly one of those evenings where I didn't have to admonish the kids to pay attention. Usually when I have a guest speaker, I'm kind of eyeing the kids, like, 'Hey, no side conversations.' I didn't have to bother with any of that.

"We had made an arrangement ahead of time," Walter recalls. "When Reggie speaks to groups, one of the things he doesn't do is come in to sign autographs. Basically, he feels that detracts from why he's there. He comes in with these pictures that he hands out. We had told the kids ahead of time, 'Don't go looking for autographs.' And they were good about that.

Our older kids, our leaders, picked up the cue after Reggie talked and led the evening discussions with the kids with their own experiences. He definitely had an impact. For a couple years after that, I still had kids talking about it."

~

One of the severest tests in White's life occurred in early January 1996, when the Inner City Church in Knoxville, which White served as an associate pastor and member of the executive board, burned almost completely to the ground, the result of arson.

The news of the torching came the day after the Green Bay Packers had waxed the incumbent Super Bowl champion San Francisco 49ers in the NFC Divisional Playoffs, a 27–17 thumping that left the team pumped for an NFC Championship Game showdown against their perennial nemesis, the Dallas Cowboys, at Texas Stadium.

Then came word of the church fire, and White's focus for the huge upcoming game was severely compromised, with heavy media attention centering around his connection to the church. Initially, White knew little more than the people with questions thrusting microphones in his face. Soon, however, racism was targeted as the likely culprit for the crime, particularly in light of the spate of church burnings that alarmingly had taken place throughout the South over the previous three years.

"This was malicious intent," said Norman Hammitt, a spokesman for the Knoxville Fire Department, who arrived at the scene of the two-alarm blaze in East Knoxville a little after four in the morning. "They wanted to see this structure burn down, and we want to find out who did it."[4]

Firefighters found ample evidence of arson: numerous five-gallon pails of kerosene, cans of Pyrodex gunpowder, and at least eighteen Molotov cocktails in quart-sized beer bottles.

Things looked a little brighter when, a mere seven weeks after the blaze, donations totaling $143,261.42 were received by White for the church's rebuilding.

"Often, the citizens would send $92 as a symbolic gesture, as this was Reggie's Green Bay Packers jersey number," mentions Gavin C. Schmitt, in his *Writings of Gavin C. Schmitt* at strivinglife.net.

However, no suspect had yet been apprehended for the crime, and in early March, the National Council of Churches of Christ, along with White, came out with a public criticism of the FBI and the U.S. Bureau of Alcohol, Tobacco and Firearms for the federal agencies' inferences that the disturbing arson attack might have been internally generated by the church's own officials. Both the Revs. Jerry and David Upton, the chief pastor and his brother, were asked to submit to polygraph tests.

White was irate at the suspicion focused on the two churchmen. He vowed to get the truth to the public, and federal authorities offered a $105,000 reward for information leading to the arrest and conviction of the person or persons responsible for the fire. Six months after the fire, the Rev. Jesse Jackson visited the remains of the burned-out church and provided a truckload of building materials for the project that were later sold for $1,500 by the Inner City pastors.

Reflecting on the ugly affair in his autobiography, White said: "In war and in football, there are rules. Invariably, some of the combatants break those rules. In football, officials are there to impose penalties and enforce the rules. Sometimes they don't do their job. Bad officiating is just one more condition of the game you have to deal with, like playing in the other guy's stadium, or putting up with bad weather, or playing with a bad hamstring or a sore knee. You gut it up and do the best you can.

"Deep in the middle of a January night in Knoxville, Tennessee, someone broke another set of rules—big-time," White continued. "The officials in that case are not refs and umpires and line judges, but police officers and federal investigators. Their job is to catch the people that broke the rules and burned the church, and to make sure that the bad guys pay the penalty for their actions. The people who torched our church are still out there somewhere. Maybe they'll get caught, maybe they won't. . . . If they don't, we'll just have to keep moving forward, keep fighting the good fight, keep working to set people free, both economically and spiritually."[5]

Two years after the fire, however, the church remained a shell. Federal agents then seized records belonging to Jerry Upton, whose personal travails were just beginning. Later that year, in December 1998, the Knoxville Community Development Corporation, which had loaned $60,000 to the Inner City Church's community development agency, sued Upton, accusing him of mixing federal grant money with his personal funds.

Four years after the fire, the church still had not been rebuilt and no accounting of the donations and insurance settlements had been issued by Upton or any other member of the Inner City Church's administration. Dark as matters appeared for Upton, things would get worse.

In a shocking culmination of events in 2000, Upton pleaded guilty to cocaine trafficking and selling a .380-caliber semi-automatic pistol and ammunition to an undercover law enforcement agent. He was sentenced to ten years in a federal prison. It wasn't the first time the erstwhile preacher had been hauled in for drug-related activity. In 1977, Upton was also convicted of selling and delivering heroin and phencyclidine (PCP).

"Reggie first met the Reverend Jerry Upton in 1980," notes

Schmitt. "He was an impressionable youth of nineteen, playing football at the University of Tennessee. Reggie and Jerry quickly became friends, cementing their relationship with the strength of their love for God and the Holy Bible. What Reggie might not have known, though, was that Upton was a convicted felon with various drug charges.

"Reggie's relationship with Upton grew over the next fifteen years, and White eventually became an assistant pastor at Upton's congregation, the Inner City Church in Knoxville. He was so impressed with what this organization could do for the community that White donated $1 million in 1995 to the Inner City Community Development Corporation, a financial branch of the Knoxville church. Less than a year after Reggie's hefty donation, the Inner City Church was damaged by fire.

"The burning was certainly intended to appear racially motivated," Schmitt continues. "One unidentified high-level investigator, speaking on condition of anonymity while the case was ongoing, told the *Presbyterian Layman* that there was 'no way white racists burned that church.'

"Reggie used his celebrity clout to call for donations, receiving many from devoted Wisconsin citizens. The National Council of Churches, who sent a total of $100,000 to the church, was under the impression the Inner City Church had been destroyed by white racists. They never bothered to question the credibility of the pastor with the criminal history and passion for driving a white Mercedes Benz."[6]

Still, White stubbornly stood by his pastor's side with consummate allegiance, even sending U.S. District Judge James Jarvis, who presided in Upton's case, a letter requesting "that you show him mercy, and if you want to sentence him, sentence him over to me and my wife. . . . This man is not a criminal; he just cares too much sometimes."[7]

First Assistant U.S. Attorney Russ Dedrick commented at the hearing that "Mr. Upton has committed a travesty on this community through his works. He held himself out to be a minister of the community, when he has destroyed human lives through his drug dealing."

The prosecutor then went on to label Upton "a manipulator who devised 'financial schemes' to bring multiple kilograms of cocaine to Tennessee for distribution. He said, 'I'm going to redevelop this city.'" Dedrick then added: "He redeveloped it all right, right around his own greed."

At that hearing, it was divulged that donations and insurance settlements for the rebuilding of the Inner City Church had totaled $912,000. The church to this day remains unbuilt.

"Reggie was an incredibly trustworthy person and naïve in some ways," says Sean Jones, White's bookend teammate at defensive end with Green Bay and now a member of the Oakland Raiders player personnel department. "He would never, ever, ever believe that the church-burning wasn't what it was. He would never believe that anyone else could've been involved."

White's stand-by-your-man defense of his onetime pastor, Jones feels, may ultimately have opened up avenues of self-examination within White. "In a quiet moment, he saw that maybe there was a part where he may have been wrong," Jones says. "And he would have to take it hard, because it wasn't the first time. He was in a situation prior to that, in some business dealings, where people may have taken advantage of his situation. After a while, it dawns on you that, 'Hey, maybe I'm being a little naïve or I am being taken advantage of.' For you to put your trust in something and then for it to turn out so different, that's just human nature."

Bowles, White's basketball coach at Chattanooga's Howard High School, when asked about the church-burning affair in

Knoxville said: "I'm going to reserve comment on that part of it. I've seen other people go in an opposite direction after awhile, because they get so confused with the Word," he said in reference to Upton.

A longtime friend and former teammate of White at the University of Tennessee, Raleigh McKenzie, isn't sure if the Upton incident changed White as a person but admitted, "I never really understood his relationship with Mr. Upton. I knew him [Upton] when he was living in the Knoxville area, you know, when he organized the church and things like that. I don't know if things went sour or if he betrayed Reggie's trust, or what. I heard about the fire, but I had no idea what came about from of it, or why."

Clark, White's friend and teammate with the Memphis Showboats, was asked if the church-burning incident had caused White to become disillusioned and colored his outlook on life. "It did, and obviously that fit a pattern in his life," says Clark. "Those were the times I saw him hurt the most, during times when friends would disappoint him. He never talked much about that, though. It was like it drained him to talk about it. He'd say, 'Just pray for me. Just pray for me.' He never did go into details about his pain.

"Obviously, I knew when a situation had taken place, when he was hurt, but he didn't talk about it. To hear it in his voice, in that tone—'Just pray for me, man. Just pray for me.'—it kind of hurt *me*."

The Eagles' Quick, recalls coming to Knoxville at his friend's request when White was starting up a community bank to assist African Americans with home loans.

"That was one of Reggie's ideas," says Quick. "He gathered a group of us from around the country, and we had some meetings down there, talking about that subject and how to move forward and do some of the things that he felt that he wanted to do in the community. A lot of poor black people who work every day rent rather than own property. One thing that Reggie wanted to do was set it up so that people who had a track record of working every day could at least get a loan to buy a house, so they could get a down payment, so they could get into a house rather than spend thirty years, forty years renting. That does a lot for people."

During that time, the Inner City Church burned.

"Yeah, I remember the whole Jerry Upton thing," recalls Quick. "I remember meeting him when I went down to Tennessee for those community bank meetings. I didn't know [about where] the money [went] . . . I didn't know that. But I'm sure a lot of those people [in Green Bay, who gave donations] backed him *because* of him. Because of Reggie. *Anybody* would have backed this guy. That's why we were out on the street."

Quick then relates about the times when White, along with his wife and sometimes even their children, would invite a couple of Eagles players to accompany them, usually on Friday afternoons, into the inner-city housing projects, parks, and playgrounds of North Philadelphia in what now is known as White's famous street ministry. For White, the time had come uncompromisingly to "kick down the doors of the devil's kingdom."[8]

A typical excursion might entail the White caravan pulling up to some park or area playground and immediately setting up a sound system from which loud music would play—an enticement to arouse people's curiosity to find out what all the commotion was about. Autographed pictures would be handed out by the players, and they might even take a turn with a broom to help in sweeping the street or become involved in some other helpful endeavor to allay any suspicions as to their presence there. White ultimately would get around to delivering his beliefs about Jesus and minister to the gathering, declaring on those "God spoke to me" occasions that the Lord had told him, "I want to take the message back to your people."[9]

This calling for White began in 1989, and he was quick to notice that not all of his brothers on the Eagles whom he asked to join him were crazy about the idea:

"The funny thing is, the guys I asked to go down in the streets with me reacted the same way I initially did: They were scared!" White noted. "'Hey, man,' they said, 'that's the 'hood! They've got gangs and guns and stuff there! Are we gonna have our limousines and a police escort?'

"I said, 'No, man. What's more, we're gonna just go in there with our trucks. No Benzes, no Jags. We're going in there to talk about Jesus, not to tie our Gospel to material wealth or give the kids in the neighborhood a lot of false hope about getting a lot of material stuff.' The guys agreed with that."[10]

Quick joined White on several of the inner-city junkets and verified White's assessment of their initial reaction.

"Sometimes it was a bit awkward, showing up in a neighborhood, in a park, with the kids," admits Quick. "A lot of people would look around, and they didn't know what to think of us. But, it was Reggie's way of trying to reach people and bring more people to God. That's what he felt his duty was: to try and bring as many people as possible to God, for them to get to know God.

"When the guy had something on his mind, he went after it. He was not afraid to speak his mind, and he was not afraid to take a position on things that he believed in his heart were the right things. Sometimes that wasn't the popular thing to do. So what if it wasn't popular? He was going to do what he felt was the right thing to do.

"Like I said, it wasn't real comfortable for me, you know?" adds Quick. "But Reggie asked me to do it. I said, 'I'm going to help you out, Big Dog,' because that's just the way I felt.

Because it was Reggie, because he asked me to do it, no question, I'm going to do it."

~

Clyde Simmons, who played the opposite defensive end slot from White when both were teammates on the Eagles, recalls those legendary inner-city ministry junkets.

"Reggie was the kind of player and the kind of person that tons of people respected," says Simmons, a mortgage banker in Atlanta today. "When it comes to that side of the respect level, there weren't a lot of things that he couldn't go and get done. People could see that he had a genuine heart when it came to that, so there was never an issue about getting it done. Going into a community to do his work was the norm for him."

~

Beyond the memory of Reginald Howard White, the day of March 25, 1998, will likely live in infamy.

That's the occasion on which White stood before the Wisconsin state legislature and delivered a wide-ranging, forty-five-minute speech touching on the many issues facing a falling America. White was encouraging about the prospects for a better world, stating that there was so much more people could do personally to better themselves and help others. He addressed high-profile problem areas and offered no-holds-barred opinions on what could be done to improve matters.

It was a courageous undertaking that for the most part urged those in the assembly to be all that they could be and more. For his efforts, White was vilified. The then–thirty-six-year-old Packer/preacher was taken to task for remarks made within the speech regarding racial and cultural stereotyping. He also reiterated his well-known, longtime stance against homosexuality. While White may have been guilty of speaking out on the controversial subjects, there was little doubt as to the overall positive tone of his message. His words were a plea for cohesion and togetherness, but the resulting notoriety stemming from the volatile reaction to his political incorrectness instead took center stage.

White later offered further clarification of his comments, but commentary in reaction to the speech ranged across the board.

"I was on stage with him," said Carol Kelso, who as a state senator helped White spearhead the Urban Hope project in Green Bay in 1997. "I introduced him that day. I knew what Reggie meant; I knew what he was saying, but I knew what he meant. This is the person who loved everyone, regardless of your race, color, creed, or sexual preference. I knew that about him. You have to look not at what Reggie said that day, but how he led his life."[11]

Dr. Ray Pritchard, senior pastor of Calvary Memorial Church in Oak Park, Illinois, strongly advocated White's position. "His overall point was very clear," Pritchard said of White's choice of words. "He wanted to show that the image of God can be seen in the full mosaic of humanity, where every group is appreciated for its unique heritage and contribution to the common good. He also spoke out against homosexuality, calling it a sin and part of the reason for America's moral decline. He went on to say 'Homosexuality is a decision, it's not a race'—which is not a popular point of view but happens to be exactly true."[12]

But other reactions were hard-hitting.

"There is another side to White that deserves exploration before his canonization is complete," said columnist/author Dave Ziron. "This side encapsulates his political ideas that spanned the gamut from the noble to the wretched. Just as White never backed down from his beliefs, we should stare them in the face and not blink away from either their bravery or bigotry."[13]

In his blog "Across the Country," C. Van Carter found another section of White's speech at the Wisconsin legislature particularly intriguing from a historical perspective. He posted these observations:

"One fascinating part of White's speech that went unnoticed at the time," notes Carter, "was his analysis of the reason American slavery was of blacks":

> *When I look at the history of America, and particularly the history of slavery, one of the main reasons that Africans were enslaved was because of economics and skin color. . . . During the time that the New World was to be built, the Europeans had to make a decision whether they were going to enslave their own. They couldn't enslave their own because their own could assimilate. . . . The only people they could enslave was the Africans because of their skin color. We couldn't assimilate, and because of our skin color, if we escaped, we were sent back to our plantations pretty much.*

"I first heard this very same and quite logical explanation for the racial basis of American slavery from a professor of economic history," said Carter. "The Rev. White was either better read than his detractors, or naturally more insightful, or both."[14]

In a 1999 article for *Focus on the Family* magazine, writer Tom Neven noted the curious immediate reaction to White's speech at the legislature:

"Members of the legislature flocked around him after the speech, eager to have their photo taken with the sports hero," said Neven in his article. "But once Reggie's words were reported in the national press, particularly his comments on homosexuality, and once homosexual activists started branding him an 'extremist' and 'bigot,' some of these same legislators changed their tune and publicly said they were 'appalled' or 'shocked' at the speech. Worth noting is that the few homosexuals in the legislature were not among those expressing shock, and Reggie said one even defended his right to say what he believed.

"Still, Reggie's honesty cost him—not just his good name, but dollars and cents, too. Several corporate sponsors dropped him, notably Campbell's Soup. And CBS Sports, about to sign a five-year, $6 million deal with Reggie to be a football commentator, backed out. [To their credit, both Nike and Edge shaving gel stuck with him.]"

Through it all, Neven said, White stood firm. "'I'm not going to sell out,' White said. 'I'm not going to back off what I know God has put in my heart to share. God owns a whole lot more than CBS could ever give me.'

"Reggie says that despite the problems he's faced since that speech in Wisconsin, he will continue to speak out," said Neven, before again quoting White: "'The greatest lesson I've learned is that too many of us don't want to suffer, and we let people back us down from what we believe in,' White said. 'The Bible constantly says that we should rejoice in suffering that comes against us.'

"'I understand that if I'm not stirring the pot up, if people are not mad at me because of the way I live and the things I say, that means I'm doing something wrong.'"[15]

After White retired from pro football following the 2000 season with the Carolina Panthers, his old high school football coach, Robert Pulliam, invited his former prize pupil to address the student body of Henderson Independent High School, an alternative school in Salisbury, North Carolina, where Pulliam is principal.

"I had him over to the school a few years ago," says Pulliam, "to speak to my students and visit a couple schools in the district. You know that old myth about alternative kids: hardcore and all that kind of stuff. Before he got here, I told him on the phone, I said, 'Now, Reggie, dadgummit, you've retired twice, and the old coach has worked every day since your high school days, and I haven't had a moment's rest. What we're going to do when you get over here, I'm going to introduce you to the receptionist, the secretary, and the assistant principal. I'm going to give you my keys, and you will be the principal for the day for the alternative school. And I'm going fishing.'

"That was a few weeks before he was scheduled to arrive. So the night before he was supposed to get in here, he called me to make sure he had final directions on exactly how to get here.

"Before he hung up, Reggie said, 'Coach, you were just kidding weren't you?'

"I said, 'What are you talking about?'

"Reggie said, 'You're not going to leave me, are you?'

"'Big sissy,' I said. 'I can't believe you! It's just a bunch of kids!'

"Well he came over and began speaking to the students," Pulliam continues. "I never will forget . . . there were two young ladies in the room, they were sisters. I don't know what in the heck prompted them to do this, but on this particular day, they came in there looking like the Bobbsey Twins. They got their hair dyed purple and all up in a 'do or whatever. Well, they made the mistake of sitting right down front, and I don't know what they were talking about, but they were whispering while Reggie was talking. And I tell you what, he cut into them.

"I was like, 'Holy *smoke*, Reggie, you could have jumped any of them, but those two right there, those are two of my rough customers.' Again, just like in the gym that day long ago at Howard, my heart jumped in my throat, and I was like, '*Oh*, boy.'

"Well he just flat gave them what for," says Pulliam. "He told them, 'Look here, the one thing you guys need to realize is respect.' He talked about respect. 'Anybody standing before you talking, you are to give them your attention.' Then he started preaching. 'Could it be that some of these mannerisms are what led you to the alternative school?'

"I'm like, '*Ohhh*, man!' You know? But before the day was over, I know he wanted to do some ministering. This is before he told me about him studying Hebrew. So I start trying to plant a seed. 'At-risk kids—that might be something. Paying visits to these schools. Just knowing you like I do, and your capacity for people, that might be something that you might want to keep in the back of your mind.'"

White often sought the counsel of others—teammates, pastors, church friends, close friends—to gain different perspectives on matters. One time Green Bay Packers teammate and fellow defensive end Sean Jones had an occasion to suggest a change of attitude, when White had become perplexed over the unrelenting pounding from questioners about his faith.

"We would have conversations about when people would ask him about why he was so serious about God," says Jones. "I was like, 'Reggie, you have to understand, people are at different phases of their walk than you are. You've got it figured out, but a lot of these guys don't have it figured out, so just be mindful of their frailties.'"

White's understanding grew—about it all. After he finally completed his long career in the NFL, the Minister began looking far beyond what he had already experienced in evangelism. The once-found man became a seeker again.

8

The Lighter Side of Reggie

In sharp contrast to the achieving player and diligent servant of God that Reggie White became and exemplified was the goofy, witty, comedic, and joke-playing Reggie, who happily showed one and all that life wasn't just about grass drills and, play diagrams. White was as much at home with a prank or a celebrity impersonation as he was with a quarterback sack or a psalm.

Engaging the lighter side of Reggie White often gave one a front-row seat to a first-rate treat. Here are some of White's more memorable offerings, as told by those who knew him best:

Henry Bowles:

"We pulled up in front of Graceland during one of our trips to Memphis. When I told them where we were, Reggie got out of the van, spread his legs, and started shaking like Elvis. 'But don't you step on my Blue Suede Shoes!' I said, 'Boy, where did you learn all these Elvis songs?' He knew every one of them.

"Another thing he would do, we'd be sitting out in the mall after eating maybe, relaxing, up there in Kingsport, I think it was, and little old ladies would pass by. '*Awwrrrhhh, awwrrrrhhhhrrrrruff!*' Then he would just look straight ahead. Little old ladies would turn around, looking to find where the dogs were coming from. Then he'd do the same thing with little kids. Oh, he loved to have fun, loved to have fun.

"I did a lot of things to try to motivate him. I used to do a lot of dancing. One day I came in dancing before the ball game, just to relax the players a little bit. One particular evening I said to the team, 'Now fellas, I want you to go out and win this ball game for the little fat man.' I guess you know everyone on the team would dare not to call me 'little fat man.' So, at halftime, Reggie said, 'Little fat man, how're we doin'?' Everybody looked at him, shocked, because of what he was saying. But I had opened the doors, so it was all right. But I said, 'Boy, you know the right time to say the right thing.' We were ahead and we were playing well. Then I said, 'I hope you know that if we were behind, you shouldn't say that.'"

Mark Burwell:

"There's a small Hilton in between our Urban Hope offices and Lambeau Field [in Green Bay]. We'd go up and Reggie would always order egg whites. One time when we had breakfast, he went up to the girls and they asked, 'What would you like?' He said, 'I'd like the egg whites.' And he looked over and they had changed the sign to 'The Reggie White Egg Special.' I've never seen such a smile on him, because they thought of him and remembered him; that meant a lot to him.

"I also remember going to lunch one day with Sara and Reggie, and they were talking about different things. They're not afraid to talk common-sense things. Somehow snoring came up. Reggie was talking about how bad Keith Byars was; he was Reggie's roommate on the road when they were with the Eagles. Of course, then it got into Reggie saying, 'Well your mother's twice as bad!' They weren't afraid to gab back and forth."

Calvin Clark:

"Whenever we had him speak for us, that was one of the things that was so impressionable about him upon kids. You bring Reggie White in and everybody knows he's the Minister of Defense—the epitome of power, strength, and speed. Then this guy comes in and he has everybody rolling from his imitations of Elvis, Bill Cosby, the Macho Man, and all these people that kids are familiar with. He could imitate jets, too, and all kinds of weird sounds.

"He had this routine where he would make like there was a war going on. He would do the fighter jets, the bazookas—you name the artillery, and he would imitate it. Everybody would just sit back in amazement, just rolling! You expected this big football player, but this guy came in and he was an entertainer. He was just the spirit of whatever presence he was in. That's why I called him "the big kid,' because he was just so full of fun, so full of life."

Chuck Dickerson:

"Oh, he was terrific. He'd put on a show, anytime, anyplace. All the time! We'd be on an airplane flying someplace, and all of a sudden you'd hear Elvis on the intercom. Course, you know, he's doin' his thing. I remember we were down there in training camp, in Florida. We were playing Orlando in a scrimmage game. Afterwards, we all ate dinner together, both teams, the coaches, we're all sitting there. All of a sudden Reggie's putting on a show for everyone in the cafeteria! We had both teams in there. Everyone was having a ball; it didn't matter which team you were on. This guy just had a love of life that was so special, it was just so special. He loved people."

Santana Dotson:

"That's what his whole day was built on. If he wasn't with the business of football or working on his spirituality, it was all about having a good time, laughter and joking. He did the [Joe] Frazier. He did the Ali. He had a Bill Clinton. His Ali was above average, but the rest of his impersonations were terrible! But that's what was so funny about Reggie; he would put his whole heart and soul into it, and you couldn't help but to laugh.

"I was talking to Bebe Winans. He said every time Reggie would call he would start his rendition of 'Amazing Grace.' Here's an outstanding, platinum-selling, Grammy Award recording artist, and every time Reggie called him on the phone—and I believe it; I can see Reggie doing it!—'*Amazing grace . . . come on, gimme what you got, Bebe. . . . Ah, that's not good enough, that's not good enough.*' That's just Reggie."

Brett Favre:

"When people think of Reggie, they think of this big man who's awesome and all-world on the field, and a preacher.

What they don't see is the guy who imitates Redd Foxx doing Fred Sanford or Ali or Bill Cosby. He's got a pretty good routine. He's also a jokester. He'll dump a bucket of ice-cold water on a teammate who's going to the bathroom. He also loves to tell jokes. Reggie has the worst jokes in the world, but we all laugh because they're so bad. I can't even remember a Reggie joke, because they're so bad, you want to forget them as fast as possible. Reggie is a lot better at telling prayers than jokes."[1]

Phillip Fulmer:

"I've seen Reggie make fun of coaches, he'd emulate coaches. He did it very well."

Willie Gault:

"His sense of humor was just incredible. He'd joke with people, but we always liked for him to do his Elvis impression. He loved Elvis and thought Elvis was The Man. He would do 'Blue Suede Shoes,' and then he'd do a great Rodney Dangerfield. Those were the two favorites that he often did."

Mike Golic:

"Oh, he had such a great sense of humor! Our locker room was so fantastic; there were so many strong personalities, and nobody was afraid to express themselves. Anything went. Reggie was as much a prankster as anybody else. He was like a big teddy bear; he had a good time. He'd joke with people; he had jokes played on him; he'd joke on people. He was a lot of fun, a regular guy.

"He was the best defensive lineman to ever play the game, but in the locker room he was just a regular guy. He would do Rodney Dangerfield and Lou Holtz impersonations. Rodney was one of his favorites. He would bust out with one whenever the situation called for it. He was always good with that. He had no problem trying to lighten up the mood a little bit."

Dale Haupt:

"He could really act sometimes, but not being a player, you know, I usually only heard about it. Sometimes he'd mess around a little bit. But when it came to football, he was serious. You've got to be that way. But everybody loved him."

Lee Jenkins:

"Yeah, he had a very playful sense of humor. He did imitations of everybody: Muhammad Ali, Bill Cosby, Hulk Hogan, Rodney Dangerfield. . . . He would call you up and be doing one of these imitations, and you might not know . . . you would think that is was the actual person calling you.

"And then he would bark like a dog. He would sneak up behind you, and at the most inopportune time, like if you were in your dorm room asleep, taking a nap before practice—and, you know, guys don't lock their dorm rooms in the middle of the day—he would open the door to the room and would crawl in or tip-toe up to your bed and then just start barking, real loud like a mad dog. Guys would just be like, 'Oh my

God!' That's kind of how he got the name Big Dog. At least that's what we used to call him."

Sean Jones:

"Any imitations that he would do—he did Elvis—Reggie was just the goofy guy. Fun-loving. For people that don't know him too good, it's kind of funny because, for a guy that was so serious, he's one of the goofiest people I've ever been around in my life. He took everything seriously with regard to football, but off the field, in everyday life, he was fun-loving. But for things that mattered to him, there was no joking. He didn't joke about God; he didn't want anyone to use profanity around him.

"He would joke about anything. He would joke about his kids, he would joke about Sara; he'd joke about anyone. To him, that was just fun. As much as he wore his religion on his sleeve at the time, he also wanted people to know that he was approachable, that he was one of the guys. We always had this joke in the locker room and out on the practice field that, anytime Reggie got upset, he would stand beside me and as he said his sentences where a curse word would come in, I would interject the curse word for him. [laughing] We kind of tag-teamed."

Johnny Majors:

"He could mock Eddie Murphy; he was a great mimic of Elvis Presley and Muhammad Ali . . . oh yeah, Reggie was a master mimic. He had a great laugh and smile. His smile would light up a stadium, much less a room. I went to his memorial service in Chattanooga, and they had some pictures of him in high school and college. That smile burst through every one of them. I said, 'God, it looks like he could come out of that canvas right now, that picture.' It was so realistic to see that smile.

"He loved to tease, and he'd tease me! One day before practice at the grass practice fields—about a four- or five-block walk; it'd take you about a good ten minutes to walk, five minutes to jog—this reporter wanted to talk to me before practice, so I said, 'I'll ride up with you in your car.' So I rode up with this gentlemen; I was sitting in the passenger side seat, and of course, I had my coaching clothes on: my whistle around my neck, and my hat. It was a nice day. We pulled up right next to the sidewalk, where the players were all passing by. When they got to within a few feet of the car, they would turn right and walk up the short steps from there to the locker room.

"So, I opened the car door and stuck my foot out on the sidewalk. I just stuck my leg out there and leaned back. I'm talking and looking toward the driver and away from where the players were walking on the sidewalk to the right. All of a sudden, this vicious dog, like a German shepherd, started 'Arrrrrrr! ARRRRRRR!' and grabbed my leg! Well, I jerked my leg and hollered. It scared the hell out of me! It was Reggie White on all fours, biting my leg, barking like a vicious dog!

"When I recovered, my heart was probably beating 150 beats a minute. It scared the living daylights out of me! I look, and there's Reggie White, this huge, 250-pound human being, rolling on the sidewalk, about to die laughing, along with about fifteen to twenty of his teammates. I mean, they were just bent over from laughing so hard. He had enough confidence that he would play a joke on me or the other coaches."

Larry Marmie:

"If you were in a room with a group of people, he was just a person that . . . people were attracted to him. He had a way of just stirring the crowd and making them laugh, and they enjoyed being around him."

Raleigh McKenzie:

"I remember when we would take the bus to the hotel—everyone would be nervous for the Alabama game—but he's going to give a Johnny Majors imitation, a Ken Donahue imitation, or give 'em his famous Muhammad Ali to get guys going. That's just his way, know you? He liked to emulate guys on the team, bring up things that happened in the past, and relive those funny stories, things like that.

"Reggie had his share of it, too. He jumped on everybody; nobody was off limits. He knew his turn. Everybody was going to try to take their shots at him as well. He was a guy that took everything in stride. He dished it out, but he took stuff, too. He was a well-liked guy for many reasons."

Hardy Nickerson:

"I heard the Muhammad Ali impression. He just loved to joke around; a bigger friend off the field. We would always joke around and stuff. He was pretty much a practical joker."

Herman Prater Sr.:

"Oh, he was more like a clown. He did a lot of imitations: Muhammad Ali, Elvis Presley, James Brown, people like that. There'd be a lot of clowning for a man his size. He liked to do stuff like that. That's what he enjoyed most.

"Some people thought I was his daddy. [laughing] People used to think I was his dad when we'd go different places. At the Super Bowl, they'd say, 'That's his mother, there. Are you his daddy?' Then they all want to know why she's so short."

Robert Pulliam:

"I remember he used to do skits throughout high school. One time, when he really started getting strong, by his junior year, I remember pulling him to the side one day. I wasn't like Reggie; I wasn't wise, but I shared with him that I had a couple friends that would pick and play with me all the time, and then they would run. This one guy, I had seen him at the corner of a hallway. He was right on me before I knew it. So I just playfully grabbed him by his throat and lifted him up. I didn't realize he had a cough drop in his mouth. When I let him go, this guy fell on the floor! I thought he was playing. Scared the life out of me!

"Now, Reggie used to do a thing where he started off imitating the Incredible Hulk, and the guys would trigger him by saying, 'Here comes Reggie's football flashback,' or something like that. He would start wiping his brow like the Hulk, and then he would begin to grab and throw people. So, I pulled him to the side, and I shared my story. 'Reggie, you don't know your own strength. Therefore, when it comes to the physical playfulness, if you were to injure someone, it would really destroy you.'

"But then also I remember—and I don't think he ever did this publicly—but back during the time when he was in high school, that Reverend Jim Jones/Guyana tragedy took place, and Reggie would do some imitations of him.

"You know, a lot of times a kid especially by their junior/senior year, they think they're grown, and someone would give them a pass and let them come down to the coach's office. But Reggie, during his junior/senior year, because of the attention of scouts, it wasn't uncommon for them to give him a pass to come see me. Anyway, I've got a physical education class, a no-nonsense class; there's a timetable, you go in, get dressed, you come out, you have a seat. You have a perfect spot that you are to be in. Everything is regimented. Even at the end of class, after you get dressed, there's no horseplay and bunch of foolishness. I had to fight Reggie, because, dadgum, he'd come down there and disrupt my whole class!

"I had a perfect class. I had a young lady at the time who wasn't real big on dress codes, but this one day she had on a black dress on with the little frills; it was almost night-club like. You know Reggie, he had a way of straightening people out and making them think about themselves, the way they presented themselves, the way they dressed. So, he comes in and starts his Jim Jones impersonation, and he says, 'And you, my sister . . . ' Sounded just like him! But the thing that was so amazing, he started talking about her, in Jim Jones's voice, looking like a prostitute! This is a high-strung girl, here. I'm like, Oh crap! She's going to want to fight! He had the whole dadgum gym in an uproar. And even *she* laughed. I can assure you, that child never came to school dressed like that again. He just had a wit about him. I believe that Reggie White, there is no doubt, could go into a dadgum prison and turn it out.

"I remember the first time he did the Elvis impersonation in public. We had what they call a Spring Fling, and actually, it was the dadgum Reggie White Show. I remember years back, the NFL, at one of the Super Bowls, featured some of his skits. But we saw it first! We had the Spring Fling, where you have all the school's talent on stage. Reggie did about every impression he had. He did the Elvis. He got the little white suit with the vest, you know, and the guitar; he was doing the Elvis singing or whatever. Then next thing you know, he's painted up all green, torn blue jeans and shirt, and now he's the Incredible Hulk! He just went on and on.

"I heard Coach Majors at Reggie's memorial service down in Chattanooga tell the story about the dog. Being a bachelor, I bought a dog; I had a Labrador retriever. When I first got the dog, it was a little bit under a year old. I was proud and so happy, because I loved dogs when I was a kid. In the summer I took my little dog over to the school, and we had weight workouts going on, and the players were doing some agility stuff, or whatever. And dadgummit, Reggie scared the daylights out of my dog. The barking. He just terrorized the dog. Well, as the dog got older, whenever Reggie stopped by my house, he *knew* that my dog would keep him at bay, because the dog never forgot.

"Reggie was always doing stuff like that. I don't remember who it was, but one time there was a lady in the gym area, and Reggie started that foolishness, that dadgum barking. He always managed to find a way to make everybody laugh, feel good about themselves, regardless of what mood they were in."

Mike Quick:

"He was the biggest kid you'll ever see. He was constantly clowning and playing around in the locker room. Pulling pranks on people. That was just the way he lived; he enjoyed making people laugh. And the nice thing was, it was easy to laugh at him. We'd poke fun at him as much as he poked fun at everybody else. He was just a fun-loving guy. The guy really loved people, people of all shapes, sizes, and colors."

~

Pepper Rodgers:

"He was a wonderful guy. He scared Johnny Majors to death, barking. He's got a great bark. But one of the most important things about Reggie, for me, was when it would start thundering and lightning, I would go stand next to him. He was a lot taller than I was, and he was a lot closer to God.

On Rodgers's condo-mate, Washington Redskins head coach Joe Gibbs:

"Gibbs lives in the same building I do in Reston, Virginia. We live on the thirteenth floor. Gibbs lives on the fourteenth. Do you know what he does? Gibbs gets on the elevator and gives little old Jewish women Christian pamphlets. [laughing] He makes Reggie White look like a non-Christian!"

~

Clyde Simmons:

"He was just a naturally funny guy. I first met him my rookie year [in Philadelphia, 1986]. He was one of those ones that went about handling the business of playing football and enjoying the game. He and Jerome Brown were like two big kids when it came to playing football and enjoying life."

9

Seeking the Truth

Seven weeks after White's sudden death from a combination of respiratory ailments that resulted in fatal cardiac arrhythmia, ESPN's Andrea Kremer interviewed Sara White, Reggie's wife of nearly twenty years. During the course of the dialogue, Kremer made a startling revelation to her audience.

"White preached the gospel throughout his NFL career . . . [and] spoke openly about his Christian faith during his fifteen years in the league," said Kremer. "Throughout his life, White had spent countless hours preaching and millions of dollars supporting the church. But after his retirement from the NFL in 2000, his spiritual journey took an unexpected turn. He began to seriously question the word he had been spreading. He stopped preaching and never set foot in a church again."

Though Kremer's news was shocking to many of White's followers, White had strongly voiced his opposition to fundamental Christianity in a national one-hour Fox Sports Net documentary, part of a series called *Beyond the Glory*, several years earlier, on March 17, 2002. In that special, White held nothing back.

"To be honest with you, I don't like people calling me a Christian," said White. "To me, as a whole, the church is doing major damage to society—most ministers won't preach against sin. I don't want nothing to do with Christianity. I do want something to do with the Jewish messiah who died for my sins, but I don't want nothing to do with Christianity.

"Most people will call this legalism," White told Fox Sports Net. "Many people will call it 'You wanting to be a Jew.' But the Scriptures call it 'Keeping the ways of God and observing his commandments.' I am trying to find out and explore what I need to do to be holy."

Prior to the ESPN piece, White, just weeks before he died, spoke more about his new spiritual path on the NFL Network. His latest journey had taken White, previously a practitioner of the New Testament, into countless private hours of studying the Hebrew language in order that he might be able to translate the original Old Testament texts himself. In addition, he made a trip to the Holy Land in 2003 to better prepare himself for his personal quest.

White was seeking the truth. More accurately, he was continuing to seek the truth. Or as White's teacher, Biblical Hebrew scholar Nehemiah Gordon, said in the Kremer interview, White "wanted to take the middleman out and get to the original message." The new direction divided his friends, with some rallying in support of the undertaking, hailing his movement into new religious realms as the work of a true seeker.

"It doesn't surprise me," says Willie Gault, former Chicago Bears-Oakland Raiders wide receiver/return specialist and White's teammate when both starred as collegians at the University of Tennessee. "That's the type of guy Reggie was. Reggie always wanted to learn; he was always trying to better himself and the other people around him. If he felt he had something he needed to learn, then that's what he did. He went out and sought the truth. He only wanted to seek truth, and that's basically what he tried to do.

"You have to try and start from the beginning and work your way through to the end, if you can," Gault adds. "It's really the only way you can become a student of the game—just like in football, basketball, or whatever. You have to know the origin of the sport you're playing. If you really want to be a theologian, it's not unlike knowing basketball: You've got to go back to Dr. Naismith and the peach baskets. If it's football, you've got to go way back to George Halas and pre-Halas. It's the origin of the game. You've got to go way back and say, 'Okay, how'd this really start? What happened? How did we do this? How did we get to where we are?' Then you can really speak intelligently about something and then teach people."

In the NFL Network interview, White surprisingly countered what was once a standard staple in his religious arsenal: the line of speech that invariably began with "God spoke to me, and He told me . . . "

On that topic, White said: "You won't hear me anymore saying, 'God spoke to me about something,' unless I read something in Scripture that I know is pertaining to what I'm feeling inside. I came to the realization that, you know what? If I'm gonna go find God, I better go find him for myself. I've got to go back and research the Scripture in its original language to see what *it* said."

In the Kremer interview, Sara White explained what precipitated her husband's decision to learn Hebrew and move down a new path. "Because he really understands the Torah," said Mrs. White, "he saw that just a little bit of distortion made a difference in the content. And that disturbed him. That's what made him learn more."

Earlier, she had stated that White had come to realize that church pastors knew what they were preaching in the pulpit was tradition, that it wasn't from the Word of God. Sara also added: "He resented the fact that people asked him to preach and speak because he was a football player."

Calvin Clark, a youth minister and White's old teammate in Memphis, concurs with Sara White's observation.

"Reggie had been disappointed so many times," says Clark. "I think it sent him out on a quest to seek the truth for itself and then to be able to equip himself mightily. He said to me one time—this was before he went into his studies and was seeking deeper—'You've had good people whom you've sat underneath throughout your ministry. I haven't had that. I'm searching for that; I'm longing for that.' And then he would speak about different people that he was beginning to subject himself to underneath. But even in that journey, he still faced and encountered disappointment.

"When he went to Israel, and he saw the rich history and culture there and the roots of our Christian faith, I think he made the decision that 'this is where I need to start.' So he began to study Hebrew. At the time, I told him that I was studying Greek. Reggie said, 'No, you need to start with the Hebrew, start with the Hebrew! That's where it all began. Start with the Hebrew!' Later on, I found out that he was also going to study Greek.

"I think the disappointment put him out on that quest, because he had been hurt by Believers also. He wanted to equip himself so that he could begin to teach, train, and disciple other young men. He said, 'We've been robbed.' I think he was speaking of the disappointments that he had encountered from different people who were close to him. I could feel his disappointment and his pain. I just always encouraged him to go forth.

"The last couple times I talked with him," says Clark, "we would be on the phone for two, three hours. He was just sharing all the different things he had learned studying the language. But he didn't want to just study the language, he wanted to experience the culture also, and he began to emulate some of that. I think that's where a lot of people read him wrong. I actually became a student in listening to him, and that had never been the case before. We used to always debate and go back and forth, but as he was sharing, man, I found myself kind of at his feet, listening—'Give me more, give me more! Send me some material!'"

Other old friends voiced confusion about White's new spiritual path, uncertain that White's passage from his tried and traditional religious beliefs wasn't evidence of someone who had become lost. White's longtime friend and former roommate/teammate at the University of Tennessee, Lee Jenkins, was one of those opposed to White's new pursuit. But in the end, Jenkins was determined not to let it undermine something of greater importance.

"Well, wow, I want to be careful how I answer this, but I want to tell you the truth," says Jenkins, an ordained minister. "It really alienated a lot of Reggie's Christian friends, and I wouldn't mind you saying that. A lot of guys wrote Reggie off, a lot of Christian guys, because they felt like he was going down a path that was not—I don't want to say not spiritually healthy—let's just say he was going towards denouncing some of the fundamental tenets of Christianity. And I was one of them. I wasn't one of the guys who wrote him off, but I was one of the guys who had some serious concerns and talked to him about it, many, many times, until it got to the point where it was dominating so much of our conversation that we decided to agree to disagree.

"I said, 'Reggie there's nothing you can do to make me not be your friend.' Sara might not have known this, but the last time I talked to Reggie—and I really wanted to tell Sara this, and I will the next time I talk to her—it was three days before he passed away. He said, 'Lee, you're one of my best friends, 'cause most of my friends have deserted me.' He wasn't referring to all his friends, because Reggie had a lot of different friends in a lot of different walks of life. He was really speaking of the people who were Christian, and who had walked with him intimately, whom Reggie had shared his journey with. Most of them didn't understand it, and neither did I. But I wasn't going to let it come between my friendship with him."

Asked if he felt the church-burning incident in Knoxville contributed to White's disillusionment with his Christian beliefs, Jenkins replies: "I think it was a combination of four things, and I literally mean four. No. 1, Reggie has always been a seeker of more knowledge. He's not one to be content with what he knows or where he is, that's just his makeup. No. 2 was probably his experience with Jerry Upton, and that whole church-burning thing. No. 3, when you are a Christian celebrity, like any celebrity, sometimes people take advantage of you. They don't mean to, but Reggie felt like some people had taken advantage of him. And then, No. 4, which a lot of people don't know but I knew, is that Reggie really missed football a lot. That void hadn't been totally filled yet, and some of his journey and passion toward [his new religious quest] was, I think, to help fill that void, to become passionate about something again, like he was towards football."

Former Green Bay Packers teammate Santana Dotson, now involved in opening fitness centers between Atlanta and his hometown of Houston that target youth and young athletes, felt White's journey to know himself was just beginning.

"It was a real big deal for Reggie," says Dotson of White's new spiritual direction. "He hadn't stopped inside a church because a lot of people wanted to use his name and notoriety. 'Oh, we have Reggie White as a guest speaker,' or 'Reggie White is delivering a message.' He didn't want that to take away from the Lord, Jesus Christ. He was focused on God when he spoke.

"Also, as he got deeper and deeper into his faith, he wanted to learn and indulge himself in the Hebrew language, just so he could get that knowledge for himself—the original text that the Bible was written in.

"He had a lot of naysayers for doing that. His thinking was: 'I need to know and figure this out for myself, word for word, before I feel comfortable enough to go back into the church, especially back into the pulpit. I need to know what this text is saying for me, before I can deliver the message to anybody else.'

"When you talk to people who really commit to Him," says Dotson, "that's really when the journey of finding one's self begins."

A longtime friend of White from his early days in Chattanooga, Herman Prater Sr., saw his old pal's new spiritual undertaking as something that was misinterpreted by many.

"I know he was studying it," says Prater, "but some people said he was deep into it. He learned the Hebrew pretty quick. It's amazing how you can catch onto it that quick. They misunderstood what he was doing, and then after they saw it on TV [the Fox Sports Net special, NFL Network interview, ESPN's interview of Sara White], they still criticized him, thinking he had gotten away from Christianity. But what he was doing was just going deeper to find out for himself. Some people said he was trying to become a Jew, but he was just going deeper into studying Christianity. It wasn't that he wanted to be a Jew. People just interpret things differently."

But White's Chattanooga Howard basketball coach, Henry Bowles, feels his former star was headed off the path. "I was a little shocked to hear that he had not been in a church and that he felt he had been deceived by some of the ministers. . . . I don't know," admits Bowles. "I don't know whether Reggie ever went to seminary or not. Sometimes, without somebody else helping, people get confused along the line of religious beliefs.

"They [ESPN's Kremer] asked her [Sara White], 'Are you Christian?' and she said, 'We're just seeking the Truth.' That kind of bothered me there. He [Jesus Christ] is not the Truth? Jesus said, 'I am the Way and the Truth.' To me, she was denying that they were Christians. They were turning down the teachings of Christ. But a lot of times people get confused with the Torah and start reading the Muslim manuscript for their religion. They have a lot of similarities there, they tell me, the Torah."

White's football coach at Howard, Robert Pulliam, wishes he had had a chance to talk with White about his evolving spiritual/religious matters before White departed.

"If I had one more chance to talk to him relative to Hebrew and the translations and so forth," says Pulliam, "the one thing that I would have said to him, which I want to hold on to no matter how smart or intelligent I get, is that I want to remain a baby in Christ as long as I can. I firmly believe that even before we are born, Christ knows who his people are. Regardless of how you walk, what you do, God's not going to let you go so far to where He can't claim you. So, relative to the Reggie White situation, where some people might say, 'I have a problem with him because he's beginning to contradict the Church,' or 'He's bashing religion,' or whatever, the bottom line, the way I see it, is that I have peace and am happy for Reggie. Because I am confident that God put a stop to whatever before it was too late. Ultimately, I cherish the memory and thought of him and firmly believe I know where Reggie is."

~

Throughout the changes that personally brought White unrest and embattlement for his parting-of-the-ways decision, his all-enveloping love for people never waned. In White, former Philadelphia Eagles wide receiver Mike Quick saw something even larger than his teammate's imposing physical size.

"As big as Reggie was physically, his heart was even bigger," says Quick. "He cared so much about people and doing for people, to the point where some people took advantage of that tenderness that was his heart. I think that probably had something to do with his position on the Church later on in his life.

"I think the search for a higher truth is a never-ending process. You're always growing in religion; you're always learning more. And as much as you know, you still don't know enough. Even for the scholars that go through all the training and spend years training, they still only know a little bit. That's just the way it is.

"He was certainly a guy in search of the truth and always a God-fearing, God-seeking type of individual."

~

While news of White's sojourn into the Torah and beyond shocked many of his oldest friends and followers, some close to White were privy to the journey's development and clearly saw the roots from which it sprang. Former Packers teammate Sean Jones remembers sharing the new direction with White.

"Reggie and I share the same birthday (December 19]—he and I and Santana Dotson," says Jones. "So, we always tried to make it a point to talk on our birthday. But prior to that, we had spoken about that [Reggie's absorption with Hebrew and the Old Testament texts] about a month or so before, in October. I always had a running joke with Reggie that he wasn't a Christian, he was really a Muslim. He and I would laugh about it. He was telling me, 'Now, Sean, remember how you were saying that? Now they're *really* going to believe that I'm a Muslim. I hear now that I'm a Muslim or that I'm practicing Judaism,' and he went on to explain that.

"Sometime ago I told Reggie that, because he was such a zealot in what he believed, he had to be careful about what he said, because people will believe that, coming from his lips, it has to be true. 'You have to really make sure that what you are saying is accurate,' I said to him, 'because everyone believes, "What's there not to believe? It's Reggie White."' He said to me: 'That's why I'm making it a point now to study the original language, so *I* can translate what was actually said, not have someone *tell* me what was said.' I found that kind of interesting.

"One of his frustrations was that he was tired of being in the position where people were telling him what to do, and then being held accountable for what he had regurgitated without having any true foundation or true perspective and knowledge of what he had been teaching himself," continues Jones. "De facto, in some respect. He felt that some people were 'basically using me to carry forth a word that I truly don't even understand. So let me go back now and understand it this way. At least if it's coming out of my mouth, I truly understand what I'm saying, where the text came from, and I have a better understanding of what I'm trying to convey.' And that's what he was trying to find.

"In prior years, Reggie was thrust into this position where people were seeking from him. He was smart enough to recognize that, 'Hey, wait a minute, I'm in a position of authority here. People are seeking the truth from *me*, and I'm not even sure what the truth is! Let me at least go and find out what the truth is. So then, coming from my mouth to their ears, it will be as accurate as I can get it out.'"

Jones then sums up White's revisiting the role again of a seeker. "If there is a flaw, it was that Reggie was not really a 'student,' from the standpoint of sitting down—and he said this—putting a book in front of him and learning. But he was *very* good at learning through osmosis. Very, very good. As things went down the road, he became this person that sat down and studied for eight hours a day. I guess the greatest measure of any person, man or woman, is your ability to see flaws and adapt. At the end of the day, I think that was probably what Reggie was best at."

~

Hardy Nickerson, a four-time Pro Bowl linebacker and sixteen-year NFL veteran with the Pittsburgh Steelers, Tampa Bay Buccaneers, Jacksonville Jaguars, and Green Bay Packers, recalls White's staggering zeal for acquiring knowledge that would assist him in the Scriptures.

"Reggie would always say, 'How can you know the Son, if you don't know the Father?'" says Nickerson, who moved to Charlotte at the behest of White about a year before White's death and is starting up a real estate agency there. "He wanted to get to know how to have a better relationship with God. He basically said, 'Okay, I'm going to put the evangelism on hold, and I'm going to go and learn and go and learn and go and learn. He went to learning the Hebrew text, because that's the oldest text that we know of, and he wanted to understand that. He would have a better feel and have a better relationship with God and understand everything that the Messiah was teaching.

A lot of people just decided, 'Hey, we're not willing to go that far.' But knowing Reggie, and knowing just a part of him—for example, as a football player—he did everything full go. When he was going after that quarterback, there was no jogging, he was going at it full bore. When he got done playing, he focused all that energy into wanting to know God and wanting to know every aspect about Him. He just dove into the Scriptures like no one I had ever seen before."

~

Urban Hope Executive Director Mark Burwell recounts an amazing and fortuitous vision that White experienced the day before he died. An account of the vision was mentioned at White's funeral by the pastor of the service, according to Burwell.

"I talked to Reggie two days before he passed away," recalls Burwell. "He was talking about how they were going to see *Fat Albert* at the theater. Then he says, 'Yep, I've been doing some Bible studies. I'm really trying to find an answer here.' That's all he really said. The next day is when he saw this vision after reading, on Christmas day itself. He saw a vision interpreting something, that there would be one unity of everything. This was said at the funeral as well. Sara knew and a few close people knew. To everybody that he talked to that day he said, 'You won't believe what happened!' This big revelation happened to him. Then the next morning he passes away.

"The whole concept [of the vision] was that all the faiths in the world were somehow going to have to come together at the end. What's amazing about this whole episode is that two hours after Reggie passed away, the [Southeast Asian] tsunami hit. Think about that. Several days or a week later, did you ever think you would have all the faiths coming together to work on a project? Reggie said he saw a sign. Now, this is before the tsunami happened! Think about that. He saw the unity; he saw that all humankind would come together.

"That was said. That was documented. That was actually talked about by the Baptist minister at Reggie's funeral," Burwell reiterates. "In Revelations, although I'm not one to know the entire Bible, it talks about part of the earth splitting. There's a total number given in there that it talks about, like a fourth of the people will die, or something. I'm thinking to myself, *This is amazing!*"

While White spoke of his vision to a few intimates on that Christmas Day, Burwell estimates the account might have spread to a larger number had not fate intervened.

"Knowing that the next day he'd be gone," says Burwell, "I'm sure he'd have gone out and talked more about it."

10

Off the Field

White's involvement with youth, community, church, and business development was so renowned that it is fair to say his reputation as an influential leader working in those areas almost matches the wealth of accolades he earned on the playing field.

His unstinting efforts to help others earned Reggie White high recognition from another noteworthy White: Byron "Whizzer" White, the late 1937 Heisman Trophy runner-up, patriot, humanitarian, and public servant, who starred briefly in the NFL with both Pittsburgh and Detroit, making All-Pro in 1940, before pursuing his more famous occupation, that of U.S. Supreme Court Justice. The NFL named its coveted Humanitarian Award after the two-time NFL rushing leader, presented annually to the player who serves his team, community, and country in the spirit of the Whizzer. White (Reggie, that is) was presented with the award in 1992. He was also named the recipient of the Jackie Robinson Humanitarian Award in 1996, in addition to the Simon Wiesenthal Center's Tolerance Award that same year.

John Opichka, former program director of Urban Hope Entrepreneur Center in Green Bay, from its origin in 1997 until June 2002, said White's devotion to helping others never wavered.

"Reggie never changed over the years," Opichka said. "He always was a very positive person, always a leader. He was a person trying to make a difference in people's lives. And that was the fun part. He was truly an impact-type person always willing to give a hand."[1]

Urban Hope, a program that White and his wife, Sara, helped initiate in 1997 to help people help themselves, has evolved to the point where the agency's instructors and volunteers now work with candidates, giving long-term assistance for startup businesses. Though in recent years White and his wife removed themselves from the program's everyday affairs, serving primarily as advisers, Urban Hope to date has yielded more than 400 graduates, helped launch more than 800 businesses, and created more than 1,100 jobs.

"A lot of people know Reggie as a football player and a legend," notes Urban Hope Executive Director Mark Burwell, "but what he has returned to the community and the seeds that he's planted here have become one of the best models in America for economic development."[2]

When Burwell first came on board, White offered suggestions.

"Reggie felt like Urban Hope really needed to get back to its mission: empowering people to entrepreneurship. He knew the concept of the free-enterprise system. Whether it was an inner-city father or a multimillion-dollar baseball or football player, they would call our office trying to get Reggie's number. Whether it was drugs or worse, they all wanted to talk to Reggie and Sara.

"Reggie's whole philosophy was to teach a man to fish," Burwell continues. "Feed him for a day, then teach him how to fish. Empowerment is so powerful. He did that with the Super Bowl team; he did that with this vision for Urban Hope. He didn't teach entrepreneurship, but he knew a lot about things, like how to be a better father. Whether someone was a multimillionaire or whether they were poor didn't make any difference. Whenever Reggie would call, before we'd talked about business, we'd talk about parenting. Both he and Sara were so concerned; they wanted me to be the best parent that I could be."

Burwell goes on to remark about the misperception that invariably dogged White's humanistic endeavors.

"Everybody wanted to put him into a social program, wanted to put him in a box," Burwell comments. "Reggie didn't care who he was helping; it could be an individual. A person making millions needs counseling as much as somebody who doesn't care. But people always thought of him as a social program. He wasn't; he was so much more than that. He was a true, true leader. A lot of people really underestimated his true vision and intelligence. I don't think there are too many people who know that."

The breadth of White's humanity, Burwell says, was in constant evidence.

"One time while I was visiting them in Charlotte, Reggie was helping a buddy drive his car; he's kind of a car lover. It was an old restored car, and the car broke down. Reggie's standing in dripping rain, on his cell phone calling for help, when a motorist comes along. The driver says, 'I think that's Reggie White on the side of the road.' The guy picks him up and Reggie gets into the car and thanks him. The man says, 'I know you're a pastor, and I'm just curious. My wife and I have been married a few months and we're in trouble. Things aren't right.'

"So, that night Sara and Reggie call me and ask, 'Mark, would you mind taking the kids out to eat? We want to meet this couple.' And they stayed with them from five o'clock till eleven that night."

The seeds of benevolent outreach, like the efforts of Urban Hope, are fueled, like many non-profits, by charitable donations. Burwell recalls an instance of one small donation that came in with a significant little tale enclosed.

"We had a nine-year-old boy who sent in two dollars in an envelope," says Burwell. "But the dad had put on the back of the envelope: 'This really was 200 pennies that my son had saved up, and I told him he couldn't do that, it wouldn't go through the mail.' But just to send to our program, he had heard about it. He's from California. It's just mind-boggling the different stories that come in here."

White spread his interests into other fields both before and after his retirement from the NFL, involving himself in a cadre of outside businesses.

He was a partner in a car dealership, Victory Chevrolet, in Mount Holly, North Carolina, near his home, and also sat on the board of the New Dominion Bank in Charlotte, where White's ability to raise money shined.

White helped the bank raise $40 million, "the largest startup in the Carolinas and Virginia," according to New Dominion Chief Executive Officer N. Bradley Thompson, who originally met White around the time that White's Urban Hope project was kicking off in Green Bay. Thompson and White were able to sell bank stock without a brokerage service through their mutual contacts and relationships. Thompson said that White's status helped considerably: "Outsiders recognized him and his reputation."[3]

With his well-developed oratory skills, White was a natural for speaking engagements, expounding on a variety of topics

JIM BIEVER PHOTOGRAPHY

The Packers retire White's jersey at a halftime ceremony during the Green Bay-Tampa Bay game, October 10, 1999. From left are White, wife Sara, children Jeremy and Jecolia, White's mother, Thelma, and Packers GM Ron Wolf.

familiar to him, including athletics, evangelism, outreach, fund-raising, and men's ministry. He could command $20,000 for appearances.

One of White's more unusual and intriguing outside undertakings was the formation of Reggie White Motorsports, a project he affiliated with the well-known NASCAR racing team of Joe Gibbs Racing, the highly successful stock car racing outfit that places well-known drivers Tony Stewart and Bobby Labonte on the track. White's alignment with JGR is an attempt to bring minorities into the sport.

"I've got to tell you, Reggie White, to me, was somebody who helped change the people around him," said Gibbs, the Pro Football Hall of Famer who came out of retirement to return to and guide the Washington Redskins during the 2004 season.

A month after White's passing, Gibbs announced, with the blessing of White's widow, Sara, that Reggie White Motorsports would live on.

According to *Milwaukee Journal Sentinel* writer Dave Kallman, "Gibbs first got to know White through football, and White sought advice from Gibbs about changing the face of racing. Last season [2004], Reggie White Motorsports, in partnership with Joe Gibbs Racing, began fielding a two-car short-track stock car team set up to help minority drivers and mechanics get a foothold in the sport. The team will continue and both cars will carry the number 92 this season in memory of White, who wore it on his Packers, Philadelphia Eagles, and Carolina Panthers jerseys. Aric Almirola, a twenty-year-old Hispanic, drives the Home Depot Chevrolet, while twenty-seven-year-old African-American Chris Bristol mans the MBNA Chevrolet.

"'We're excited about that,' Gibbs said on continuing White's vision. 'It's helping the sport and taking it in a direction we think it needed to go.'"[4]

On April 9, 2005, Bristol, from Columbus, Ohio, won his first race of the season, the first African American in the fifty-five-year history of Hickory Motor Speedway to claim victory. Of his landmark win, Bristol said: "It's just unbelievable to win at Hickory; this track is legendary."

Almirola, from Tampa, Florida, claimed his second victory of 2005 in the Late Model Series, also at Hickory, on May 7.

Rockwell Automation sponsors JGR's diversity program and both drivers. "We were excited when Joe and J. D. [Gibbs] told us about their plans, and we're pleased to be able to partner with JGR and Reggie White on such an important initiative," said Jay Lee, director of business communication for Rockwell. "We believe it will pay dividends, both inside and outside the NASCAR community, for years to come."[5]

11

Remembering Reggie

It seems everyone has a favorite Reggie White story.

Players who knew his intensity and talent on the football field regale listeners with remarkable tales of his athletic prowess. Friends knew the "teddy bear" side of the big man, while acquaintances in charitable and business endeavors cherish the interaction they had with him. Some, like fans, witnessed what White presented on the playing field or perhaps met him in a church or school setting. Each and all, regardless of their level of interaction, came to treasure with genuine appreciation the gift that was Reggie White.

Henry Bowles:

They're going to name the gym in my honor. I really wish that Reggie could be there for that occasion. But I'll just have to meet him on the other side. I'm going to have a moment of silence for all of my fallen warriors. Because without all of those guys and their sacrifice, like the song says about Jesus,

"Without Him, I wouldn't be anything." Without my players, I wouldn't be what I have gotten to be. I'm grateful to them. [The Henry Wesley Bowles Gymnasium at Chattanooga's Howard High School was dedicated on February 27, 2005.]

Mark Burwell:

Keith Jackson would always say about Reggie, "Reggie, he was so tight." I think they even had a little blurb on it on ESPN, about how he would always be the last one to pick up the check. But you know something? They'd look at him and say, "But you've got the biggest pockets." Then Reggie would say, "Well, you get a paycheck, don't you?" That's Reggie. But then, two days later, he'd write them a $50,000 check to their foundation. That's the kind of guy he was. He believed in that.

Calvin Clark:

You mention the word fallen with Reggie, it just don't compute. A risen warrior is the way I would put it. He got drafted all over again. That's my little brother.

He invited us all over to his house one night to see the fights. We had a Bible study that met every Friday that rotated around to different players' houses. There was a big fight—might have been Hearns-Hagler—he had this big satellite dish, and he was promised that he would be able to get the fight. So, we're all over at his house, we're anxious to see the fight, and of course, it never came in. He was moving around the house with the remote trying somehow to get it to come in. Finally, he went outside and began to tilt the big satellite dish. That was one of the funniest evenings that we had, because he's got all these people over there all wanting to see the fight. We never did see it. We just wound up laughing and joking him all night.

Reggie was the one that I envied so much, because his gifts were just a perfect fit for youth ministry. And that's what I do: youth ministry. I wish that God had blessed me with all the talent, imitations, etc., that he blessed Reggie with, because that's what makes you approachable to youth. It opens the great doorway for you to minister to youth. Reggie always had that innate within him, just a God-given talent. So, I always looked up to him and envied him, in that sense, in wanting to have his personality. But I'm working with youth here in Denton [Texas], discipling young people from ten to eighteen, and also adults. Been here for ten years now.

I just enjoy talkin' about him. He was like a little brother to me. We became such good friends over the years, and his wife, Sara . . . well, I owe her my life. She hooked me up big-time. [laughing] (NOTE: Sara introduced Calvin and his future wife, telling her friend Devorah one day, "I just met your future husband.")

She had always tried that [matchmaking Devorah and Calvin], and I said, "No, no, no, no, no." I called at their house one time, and she said, "Oh, C. C., I'm glad you called! I don't want you to say anything, but I want you to hear this: I met your wife today. I just want you to meet her." Later I would say, "Reggie, there's a prophet in your house!"

So, sure enough, she flew me up. She was giving Reggie a surprise birthday party, and he didn't know I was coming up. Sara wanted me to emcee it. That's where I met Devorah. She and Sara worked together in this hospital, where Sara was a volunteer; Devorah worked there. That would have been in 1988. She had Reggie introduce her to me. My wife would kind of housesit for them at times and help them out with the kids. It was kind of funny, 'cause I kind of did the same thing when Reggie left for the Eagles. He had to leave and Sara was pregnant. I would be over there helping Sara sometimes. I would be just *pining* for when Reggie was going to call, so that I could answer the phone, "Rent-A-Dad. Can I help you?" We loved to tease him: "Boy, you're abandoning your family for football! What's wrong with you!"

At the funeral, after we left Charlotte, driving up to the grave site, we had to go through two or three small towns. They had the local sheriffs and the highway patrol block off the main entrances as we drove by. At the intersections, there were policemen standing there with their hands over their hearts. They made it seem like you were in a movie.

Reggie and Sara are very special, dear people. Like I said, I owe my life and my ministry to them, because my wife has been such a helpmate to me in ministry. I wouldn't be freed up to do what I'm doing, apart from God's gift of my wife. Sara was just a big plus for Reggie. She kind of warded off a lot of the wolves around the attention that he was getting. You know, Reggie didn't realize how big he was in the public's eye. He was not aware of how people would try to get close just for their own advantage. Women are good at seeing through that kind of thing.

Sara's a sweet, sweet young lady, and my heart aches for her. She went through the funeral so strongly. I was just amazed at her strength.

I saw Bruce Smith standing there, tears coming down his eyes. Here's a guy who in his own right was a great defensive lineman, but to see tears coming out his eyes just showed the amount of respect that Reggie carried in the NFL and how much respect those guys had for him. It just humbled you to see those guys weeping over their lost comrade.

Chuck Dickerson:

Reggie had a type of naïveté that was a tremendous pleasure to experience. He was a guy that believed and felt all the good things, the adages about the game, the things you say about people. If you said, "Boy isn't this game fun?" Reggie would be the first guy to say, "Yeah, boy, football's really fun!" Or if you'd say, "Wasn't that a really nice guy that stopped in?" Reggie would say, "Yeah, what a terrific guy!"

That was Reggie all the way. He was a guy who wanted people to be happy around him and to experience this feeling about the love of life that he had. Of course, he personified that in all the things that he tried to do throughout his lifetime, being a very religious person.

Now, in my case, I wasn't involved in that part of his life. That was something that was aside from the football end of things. But you can't help but be a part of it, because you're a part of Reggie. You can't be around Reggie White without being a part of him. That's just who he was, you know?

Over the course of time Reggie, because he's very important to the game, will always be remembered. These articles and books are important things to let young people, who really never had an opportunity to know anything about him, see what it's all about to be not only a great football player but a great human being.

Willie Gault:

Reggie and Lee Jenkins and I were onetime roommates [at the University of Tennessee]. We had a dorm that had connecting doors next to each other, and we were there for two or three years together. We had great times. And, of course, I played against him in the National Football League and remember him chasing me on reverses when I played with the Bears and he was with Philadelphia.

One story that sticks out as much, if not more: Reggie and I were in the *Superstars* competition together down in Miami. We were there a couple of years together. One year, I had to play Reggie in the finals of the tennis competition. I was a pretty good tennis player at the time, and Reggie was not a good tennis player. I don't know how he got to the finals. I beat him either 6–0 or 6–1. I think I let him win a game. I went over to shake his hand afterward, and he tried to hit me and chased me around the tennis court. It was really funny. We had a good time with it. It was really cool.

I miss the camaraderie with the guys, and I miss the big games. It's a part of life. Football's a great sport. I really have nothing but fond memories of it. I have great relationships, like the ones I have with Reggie and all my other teammates—Tim Brown [with the Raiders], and the Bears' Mike Singletary, and all those guys. It's a fraternity that lives forever, with the camaraderie and respect that you have for each other. It takes a certain amount of dedication, perseverance, patience, and a lot of prayers to play that game, and you have to be a pretty smart guy to know all those plays. I think we who have played the game understand it and know it and respect it. So, that's a good thing.

Reggie meant a lot to a lot of people. His death was an unfortunate thing, but as you can see from his service and all the people that came to his funeral to express their sorrow and best wishes for Sara, he was a great friend. Sara's lost a husband and his mother's lost a son, which you never can replace, but we are all in a much better place for having Reggie here on earth with us than not to have had him at all.

I call Sara and his mother periodically, just to talk to them and say hello. Nothing can really, really help, but just a friendly voice sometimes can feel good. The loss is on a magnitude that we can't imagine. My mother went through it, because my sister passed away about three years ago. It's just a tough thing for a parent to bear, the loss of a kid. It's tough for a kid who loses a parent, too, but for a parent to lose a child is bad. It's so unexpected.

If someone's been sick and they're in the hospital, and they've been diagnosed, and they're older, you know—seventy, eighty, ninety years old—you're like, "Okay, I can deal with it." But the loss that comes from someone one day being jovial, happy, and a person that's bigger than life, and then the next day they're gone—it's just such a shock to everyone.

Mike Golic:

The one thing about Reggie that everybody knew was that he didn't swear. Reggie never uttered a bad word. He didn't mind if you did it, if you swore. But he didn't swear and didn't want anybody to swear at him.

We were playing the Detroit Lions, and there was a tackle who basically held Reggie on every play, and Reggie told him to knock off the holding. This guy went into a swearing tirade against Reggie that had us all stopping in our tracks, looking, and just basically laughing on the field. All Reggie was saying was, "Don't you cuss me! Don't you cuss me!"

Well, with this guy, it just egged him on. He was calling Reggie every name in the book. We were like, "Oh my God, what is this guy doing?" Finally Reggie just looked at him and said, "Jesus is coming. Jesus is coming."

Reggie walked back to the huddle. We break the huddle for the next play, and Reggie lines up over the guy. This is a preseason game, so the rest of us on the D-line—like me, Clyde Simmons, Mike Pitts—we could care less what happens on the play. We're watching Reggie. He gets in his stance, and the quarterback is in his cadence. Right before the snap you hear Reggie say, "Here comes Jesus!"

The ball was snapped, and Reggie hit this guy in the chest. And that's a big man; this guy is about 6–7, 290. Reggie just hit him in the chest, hoisted him, and threw him into the quarterback. Reggie tackled the quarterback *with* this guy! So the guy's lying on the ground, and Reggie looks over at him, points a finger at him and says, "Don't you ever cuss me again!" and turns around and walks away. I was just like, *Whoa!* It was hilarious. Reggie's abilities on the field were unmatched. God forbid you angered him. That was the wrong thing to do.

***Lee Jenkins*:**

Reggie is known as a man. Whether he's right or wrong, as long as Reggie believes in it, he'll die for it. I mean, that's just how he is. And you have to admire that in people. There's a little saying: "People who don't stand for nothing will fall for anything." But, nonetheless, Reggie is the kind of guy who didn't have any gray areas in his life. He was either for it or against it.

Reggie and I had to speak at a church over the Christmas holidays while we were at Tennessee. Actually, we were preparing for a bowl game. This was Reggie's sophomore year and my junior year, and a church had invited us to speak to some kids. On the way there, Reggie said, "You know, all these kids are thinking about Santa Claus." Reggie's message, so to speak, was supposed to be about the importance of Christmas. And so, Reggie said, "If I'm going to really tell these kids about Christmas, I have to tell them the truth."

I said, "What do you mean, Reggie?"

"I have to tell them there's no Santa Claus."

I said, "Reggie, you can't do that! That's not your job, and the kids are going to be crushed; the parents are going to be crushed." I said, "Reggie, please don't do it."

But, see, Reggie is either right or wrong. And he doesn't do real good with little nursery rhymes or fairy tales. He's not good with stuff like that. So, the bottom line, Reggie agreed with me. "Okay, Lee, I'm going to try not to say anything."

Of course, he's up talking and gets on a roll. He looks over at me and says, "Lee, I *gotta* say it." So, he tells the kids: "Kids . . . "

He did it in a tactful way, but it was still devastating. These kids were like, Oh, man! I mean, obviously, some of the parents were a little upset. And some of the kids were crushed. But overall, Reggie didn't mean to hurt anybody. Reggie is just the type of guy, who's like, "Hey, you invited me here to speak about Christmas." And I think the subject might have been "The True Meaning of Christmas," something like that, so they wanted him to talk from a Christian perspective. I mean, obviously that's what Christmas is. And so he took it a lot further probably then what they wanted, by telling the kids there's no Santa Claus.

So, I was up there sitting behind Reggie while he was talking. And I was, Oh God . . . I just put my head down, 'cause I felt so bad for those kids. There are about forty or fifty kids who are probably grown now, whose first experience of finding out there was no Santa Claus was Reggie White.

Johnny Majors:

He is the most impressive physical mass of humanity I have ever seen come in my door. When he was playing football for Memphis, he walked in my door once and I thought, Good gosh amighty, can anybody be that broad, that big, tall, all in one package? I was astounded, I really was.

Reggie was a natural leader and a spokesman for the players. He'd get up and say something to the defensive linemen or to the team at halftime or during practice—"We're not doing what we need to do; let's get this thing going right!"—that kind of thing. He was just so massive in his physical structure of build, and he had such a vivacious nature and personality full of vitality. He just lit up the whole area when he spoke, because his eyes flashed whether he was smiling or laughing or whether he was serious or competing.

They say that the eyes are the windows to the soul, and I'll tell you, Reggie White's eyes were the windows of his soul if anybody's ever were. If he was upset at practice, or if he was ready to whip somebody who hit him low or clipped him, his eyes fired up. His eyes also had great compassion in them. Great, great eyes, besides having his phenomenal physical ability. He was an outstanding person and had a great sense of humor.

~

Larry Marmie:

He was such a terrific person. He grew and matured into his professional football career and his family. Sara and he, of course, weren't married at that time, but that's where they began [at UT]. What a wonderful family it developed into, which didn't surprise me or anyone else.

That was a very important part of my life and my coaching career, having had a chance to be around him. I certainly was a better person for having had a chance to know him. We'll miss him. A lot of people will miss him. But those people who had a chance to know him just a little bit, on a more personal basis, certainly will miss him.

Raleigh McKenzie:

He was adored by a lot of people. If you were just one of the tutors at Tennessee, one of the professors, or a friend who was a star, or a friend who was a walk-on, he treated everybody the same. He joked with everybody and gave everybody the feeling that we're all here for a purpose, that we're all in this thing together. I think he did that professionally, too. He was one of the only ones who could really talk and joke around with Buddy Ryan back with the Philadelphia Eagles.

Everywhere he went, he drew a lot of people to him. Once he got to Philly, he was a big, major factor in them becoming winners. And at Green Bay, I think his attitude definitely rubbed off on Brett Favre and the rest of those guys. They'll tell you, too, that his approach to the game, his lightheartedness, and his humor kept them going. A lot of people were drawn to that. If they were really uptight about something, it was "Hey, let me hang around Reggie, he'll get me away from that."

Hardy Nickerson:

More than the football player, it's the Christian side that I knew most of Reggie White. He genuinely cared about people and wanted to see people better themselves. Especially with his efforts in charity things, such as Urban Hope. He genuinely wanted people to just have a better life than what they had. He worked tirelessly at that.

I also saw the minister side of the Minister of Defense. He genuinely cared about people, not only as football players but as persons. He would share that tirelessly, teaching guys how to be a father and a husband—just things that you don't get from anybody everyday.

Herman Prater Sr.:

We went through a lot and talked a lot. I went to the Super Bowl in '96 and took pictures for him. I've been taking pictures for him since he was in the ninth grade. I'd just spoke with him on his birthday before he died. I couldn't believe it, really. It hasn't sunk in yet. It's rough, you know. I told his mother we'd have to get through it together.

Robert Pulliam:

I remember telling Reggie when I went to Chattanooga to coach that I still had some yearning to play football. After I accepted the job in January, when I had been on the job a couple weeks, I messed around and signed a free-agent contract with the Cleveland Browns. I didn't tell anybody. I just wanted to go to camp and prove some things to myself. I was going to come back and do what I said: coach.

So I went to camp, messed around there, and things started going *too* darn good. It looked like I had a chance to stay around, but those little kiddies at Chattanooga Howard High School haunted me. So, I ended up talking to the Browns' head coach, who was Forrest Gregg at the time, telling him of the promise I had made to those kids. He had invited me to come back and reclaim that contract come January of the next year. But in the meantime, I messed around and met that little scoundrel named Reggie White.

Ol' Reggie messed around and wired me. He messed around there and got word that I wasn't really planning on being there at Howard that long, that I was going to go back and pursue a career in pro football. He asked me during the final recruiting process, he said, "Well, Coach, if I come to your school, are you going to get me here just long enough to get me in the door, and then are you going to leave me?"

So I had to promise him and his teammates: "No, I won't leave. I'll give you my word. Only thing that could get me out of here is if the dadgum principal fires me."

Certainly, looking at Reggie and that group at that time—it really was an at-risk school—it's kind of been my lifeline, the thing that really sustained me, being able to work with and try and find a way to support and help kids. As I told Reggie a few years ago, every now and then I think I'm tired and I'm about ready to retire. I'd say, "Reggie, I want to be like you!" [laughing]

But then a new year comes along, with a group of new challenges with students, and next thing you know, I start feeling I'm about ten years younger than I am.

I kid with my sons. I would tell them, before Reggie passed away, "That guy right there is the reason your dad is not an ex-NFL player."

I remember some years ago there was a tickertape parade, banquets, and all these things. I had the privilege of meeting Buddy Ryan and so many other folks down in Chattanooga. I started thinking about Reggie. This guy has lived! I didn't understand at the time. I thought people started celebrating long after you had retired, and in some instances, long after you were gone. I just thought it was so amazing. As I reflect back, all these celebrations were done, and Reggie had a chance to witness it and be in the mix of it.

But still God was in control, and He had a plan. When I first got the news, and throughout the day as it was confirmed, I'm getting a little angry. I'm thinking, *Dadgummit, the boy has not had a chance to enjoy the fruits of his labor!* I fully expected Reggie to go on and on and on. Growing up, he didn't have a whole lot. And to be at a point where now he was retired from football, where he could finally enjoy . . . *God, it's so unfair that You would call him at this time*. I'm apologizing to God, because I know He knows best, but for that moment, I was upset. My gracious! Even now, to the point where I'm upset, I'm like, "Wait a dadgum minute. This guy was supposed to bury *me*!" I was just totally whacked out with the whole situation. But I just thank God that I have peace with it now, and that I'm again able to totally trust that He knew what was best.

***Mike Quick*:**

If you know the guy, you love him. Spend anytime with the guy, you love him. I do this little football camp down in my hometown. As big as Reggie is, but because we were friends, I called him up: "Reggie, I'm doing this football camp."

Reggie: "Oh yeah, what's the date?"

And there are guys that aren't even close to Reggie's status that I asked to come down, and they thought it was such a big deal and such an inconvenience and "How much money are you going to pay me?" I never once got that from him. Just "When is the date, and when do you want me to be there?" And he was so good with the kids. It was such a nice time.

When you talk about Reggie, I think he was a great example for all of us in terms of how to handle your family, how to treat your wife, how to treat your kids. We teased him a lot about Sara, you know, running the house. We always kidded him, saying that Reggie had a track out around his house. He ran *around* the house 'cause Sara sure ran the house. We always teased him about that. And we asked him if he had enough money for lunch, if Sara gave him money for lunch, or how much allowance did he get, 'cause we all knew he took his check home and gave it to Sara.

As you get older, you get wiser; you understand. He had it, what we searched for. What we're learning about now, as older guys, Reggie had that already. He knew how he was supposed to manage his house. You know, I think he would have left this world with a whole lot less had Sara not been so involved in the house finances, and such, 'cause Reggie's heart was so big he would have given everything away.

Clyde Simmons:

I can tell you one thing to me that stands out about Reggie. He always stood up for what he believed in, whether it was popular or not. A lot of people just talk about the same things, but he has always stood up for what he believed, whether or not his decision was the one they did or didn't want to hear. He never had any qualms about what he had to do.

***Tony Walter**, on White's gratis appearance at a community service program for kids at St. Anne's Episcopal Church, in De Pere, Wisconsin:*

He came in, and of course the kids. I mean, it was already something that they were quite excited about. The only thing he asked of us was would we feed him and his family. We were serving a spaghetti dinner. After he spoke, I had our high school seniors come up and escort him up to the front to get his spaghetti. They were just blown away, because he had a plate of spaghetti that was enormous. I was thinking at the time, Oh, that's *way* too much! And, my gosh, he went into that and scarfed it down. The kids were just gathered around him; they all wanted him to talk to him.

FAN FAREWELLS

***Ron Burnis**, Zeeland, Michigan:*

The plays he made as a Packer are too many to count. The lives he touched, probably the same. However, my best memory of Reggie White came a couple years ago. I attended a "Lombardi Legend" event along with my friend Kevin Talley. Reggie became the first member not to have played for Coach Lombardi. He was among Starr, Taylor, Kramer, Wood, etc. Maybe greater than all of them, you could never tell. Kevin and I noticed how honored and humble he seemed to be while being part of such an awesome group of Packer legends. We had our picture taken with the entire group, including Reggie. I'm sure all who attended the event remember how nice Reggie was, and I value that picture more then ever.

Gary Price, *Negaunee, Michigan:*

My personal memory of Reggie was when I asked him on Larry McCarren's locker room show if he would go into the Hall of Fame as a Packer or Eagle when he retired. At the time, he said he'd have to think about that after his playing days were over. I believe he later told Bob Harlan that he would indeed be a Packer NFL Hall of Fame entry. Also I will never forget him running around Lambeau with the NFC championship trophy and waving to all the fans. It only took him six seasons to become one of the all-time most-remembered greats in Packer history.

Bob Anderson, *Ridge Manor, Florida:*

We were playing the Vikings. The QB faded to throw a pass and [wide receiver] Cris Carter was, for some reason, supposed to block Reggie. Reggie picked him up and threw him, underhanded, back into the QB, somewhat like a bowling ball. The look on Carter's face when he saw Reggie coming was like a deer in headlights. Being Reggie, he helped Cris up and gave him a pat on the back. I'll never forget that play.

Peter Anathan, *Waukesha, Wisconsin:*

A friend and I visited the old Packer Pro Shop, and I was watching a TV monitor which was featuring Reggie White. My friend said, "Hey, there's Reggie!" and I responded, "Yes, I see him." My friend said, "NO, he's right there!" pointing outside. I suggested we go give him some money for his church that recently burned down. We went outside yelling for Reggie to stop so that we could give him some money. He, however, said he needed to run to pick up his kids. He began to drive off but then stopped and waved us over. He accepted the money and offered us autographs. We actually declined the autographs, as that wasn't our intent. He said thanks and then drove off. A situation like this is found in Reggie's book. Maybe it is us, and then again, maybe it isn't. But who cares? It was a great encounter, and I will always remember it.

Jerry Chapa, *Brillion, Wisconsin:*

Reggie came to speak at my high school in Milwaukee in 1996. Over time I have forgotten the words he said, but I have not forgotten the look in his eyes and the compassion in his voice. He spoke about effort, will, fortitude, and success. He stressed the importance of education. I had an opportunity to speak with him briefly that day, and I remember him being very gracious and a gentleman. I took his message and have carried the theme of his talk throughout my life. Sadly, his words were not received by all the students, but they were well received by me. May he not be forgotten by all, and may he rest in peace.

Greg Stielstra, *Grand Rapids, Michigan:*

My fondest memory involves Reggie on videotape. I went to the NFC Championship Game against Carolina, on January 12, 1997, even though I didn't have a ticket. My friend and I snuck in at the start of the fourth quarter when an ambulance attendant opened a gate on the east side of Lambeau. We were standing in the aisle at the 50-yard line on the east side of the stadium at the two-minute warning. A strange calm fell over the stadium. Television had cut away for beer and tire commercials. Action on the field had stopped. The Packers' lead was insurmountable and, along with everyone else, I was overcome by the realization they were going back to the Super Bowl for the first time in twenty-nine years.

I thought back to a Sunday night in the 1970s when, as a young boy, I had cried myself to sleep because the Packers had lost and I knew my friends would tease me the next day. "Why do you root for the Packers anyway? C'mon, switch to another team and we will leave you alone," they would say. But I couldn't. I had to be true, and I knew the moment was sweeter because I had never wavered. I had stayed the course, and this was my reward. And then I realized that my experience was a metaphor for the Christian life. Every Christian has opportunities every day to "switch teams." The temptations are endless, but by staying the course, our reward will be sweet.

While I was pondering that, they played a video on the Jumbotron in the north end zone. It was a collage of Reggie's highlights set to a soundtrack of Reggie singing "Amazing Grace." As it played, the entire stadium began to sing along. I will never forget the experience of singing "Amazing Grace" with a stadium full of Packers fans led by the great Reggie White. Who else but a man of his faith, stature, conviction, and irresistible charisma could have that affect? [What a] wonderful memory Reggie gave me.

Peter and Debe, *Franklin, Wisconsin:*

God bless you, Reggie. God must have big plans for you!

Ken Webster, *Houston, Texas:*

I remember the time I met him at the Santana Dotson Foundation in Houston. It was shortly after the infamous speech he gave to the Wisconsin state legislature. As an educator trying to make a difference in the lives of students, I felt compelled to give something back to Reggie. Although the comments were inappropriate, I felt the intentions were good and that the media "spun" them out of control. I thought a long time about what I, a lone Packer fan in Houston, could do to make a difference in his life.

I decided to share a prayer that was read at a Black History Month celebration in the high school I worked at. The prayer centered around the theme of race—the point being God didn't see individual races; he only saw his children.

I remember feeling a little nervous as I approached him at the dinner but felt calm as soon he cracked a smile and greeted me with that deep, raspy voice of his. I gave him the prayer, never knowing what, if any, impact it ever had. But I know his life impacted mine, and for that I am grateful. Even though he no longer walks with us on earth, I know his spirit continues to watch over us. His words and deeds will forever influence us—Packer fan, Eagle fan, or member of the human race. His work is in our hands, and we should all continue to seek meaning in our lives, deepen our sense of faith, and help our fellow members of society. Rest in peace, Reggie.

Jim Meyer, *Manitowoc, Wisconsin:*

My favorite memory of Reggie came from 1997, the week before the Super Bowl in New Orleans. My wife and I went into Reggie's store in Green Bay. Eugene Robinson was in there promoting a CD he and another performer had just released. Eugene was playing his saxophone, and his partner sang. They did a few songs and then were shaking hands and signing autographs.

Reggie walked in. Somebody told him he should do a song with Eugene, but he declined, saying he didn't know any songs, when someone from the back of the store yelled out, "Hey, Reggie, how 'bout 'Amazing Grace'?" He smiled and agreed to sing. So, in that small store, filled with about fifty other Packer fans, I joined arms and sang "Amazing Grace" with the greatest defensive end to ever play football. I will never forget that moment.

Brice Anderson, *Mechanicsville, Virginia:*

The arrival of Brett Favre in 1992 and Reggie White in 1993 coincided with the advent of sports bars and NFL Sunday Ticket. That meant that, finally, Packers fans outside Wisconsin could be certain of seeing our games every week. A core group of us, and later, our wives, and even later, our progeny, gathered most Sundays at Mulligan's to watch our championship team form itself and march inevitably toward the Super Bowl. My everlasting memory will be of my friend Doug bellowing toward the Minnesota Vikings fans in the room after another sack: "Reggie has landed on the Moon!'"

Jim Williams, *Green Bay, Wisconsin:*

While Reggie was playing in Green Bay, he made an appearance at the National Railroad Museum in Ashwaubenon. My son Jameson, about eight at the time, was there. At the conclusion of the appearance, Reggie signed some autographs. As Reggie was leaving, apparently having signed as many as he could, Jameson finally got near him. He asked for an autograph, but Reggie was making his way out. Upon hearing the request, Reggie asked my son, "How about a hug?" He didn't get the autograph but got much more from No. 92. What other athlete would ever make such a counteroffer? From what other athlete would such a gesture seem so natural?

***Amanda**, Milwaukee, Wisconsin:*

What do you do when your hero has died? I have always looked up to number 92. As a female football player, he provided me great inspiration. I watched him take things in stride, and in turn was able to do the same thing. . . . He was an extraordinary man who will greatly be missed.

***Beth Riggs**, Woodland, California:*

During the 1994/1995 school year, I taught in Green Bay. Mark Brunell was scheduled to come to the school for an assembly. Apparently, something came up, because he was unable to make it. However, when the children were assembled, another Packer came to take his place. It was Reggie White! He said he didn't want to disappoint the children, so he arranged to come for Mark Brunell.

The children were completely enthralled by Reggie, as was the staff. I was very touched by the fact that this man would care so deeply about how some children would feel that he arranged to come himself. It was an honor to listen to him speak to the children motivationally and to shake his hand. Reggie White may have only walked the earth for forty-three years, but he accomplished more positive things in that time than most people do in a lifetime of great length.

~

***David Eisner**, De Pere, Wisconsin:*

He was the whole package, on and off the field.

~

***Ann Schmidt**, St. Louis, Missouri:*

I was a second-grade teacher at Elm Grove Lutheran School in Elm Grove, Wisconsin, during the late 1990s. My students and their families were, of course, all avid Packer fans, as was all of the teaching staff. It was easy for us to love all of the players on the Packers, but Reggie White was the most loved and revered. Several times, my young students wrote letters of encouragement, expressing their faith to Reggie. Each time we wrote, we received a response from his wife on behalf of Reggie, a letter of encouragement to stay strong in their faith along with an autographed picture to hang in our classroom. Reggie White was our hero, and I know that the memories of his heroics in Green Bay and the example of a faith-based life made a lasting impression on a group of impressionable elementary school students.

~

***Charles Nusberger**, Baltimore, Maryland:*

My cousin Mike Salzman and I used to imagine ourselves as players, playing in the front yard of his parents' Grafton home.

Mike was in a wheelchair but never complained about it. As he became more ill, he grew more and more a fan of Reggie's. After he died, he was buried with a jersey with the number 92 on it, pictures of Reggie, and, if I remember correctly, a football in his hand. I met Reggie at a thank-you service when the state helped out his church after it burned down. I told him how much he meant to my cousin in his final months and days. Then we prayed together, and at that moment, I was filled with the Holy Ghost. Reggie was with me the whole time, and that is a day that I will never forget.

Bob Smith, *Waukesha, Wisconsin:*

With the first pick of the Heavenly Football League draft, the Holy Trinity select . . . Reggie White, Minister of Defense. God Bless, Reggie, you will be missed.

Kathy Schultz, *Lincoln, Nebraska:*

I'll always remember his smile and the shine in his eyes. The good Lord must have needed him bad. Now Brett's dad will have someone to watch the Packer games with. Thanks for the memories, Reggie!

(*The above tributes were collected from* "Tributes to Reggie White," *http://www.jsonline.com/packer/news/dec04/reggiewhite-forum.asp;* "Fans share favorite memories of White," *http://www.packersnews.com/archives/news/pack_19197320.shtml; and* "Readers recall on-, off-the-field memories of White." *http://www.packersnews.com/archives/news/pack_19229508.shtml.*)

FAREWELLS FROM THE NFL

***Eugene Robinson**, Packers safety (1996–97):*

[At the funeral service] Keith Jackson talked about Reggie the way we know Reggie. He talked about Reggie eating up all the food. How he ain't gonna pay for nothin'. All the stuff that we know. And he did it in such a manner that it allowed us to go ahead and be his friend again and to celebrate him again. I thought Keith did a marvelous job of conveying to us who "Big Dog" was as far as being funny. He'd break out in an Ali impersonation. He'd hit you in the back with a wet bar of soap as you're coming out of the shower. That was Reggie.

***Larry McCarren**, Packers center (1973–84):*

I guess the real message is to carry on Reggie's message, which was one of faith.

***Ryan Longwell**, Packers kicker (1997–):*

I thought that Reggie was a guy that could go across so many different boundaries. He broke down the stereotypical athlete. You could have a heart. You didn't have to swear. You didn't have to beat your head against a locker, but you could still go play with passion and live your life with passion, too.

Brett Favre:

He may have been the best player I've ever seen and certainly was the best I've ever played with or against. Off the field, he did so much for so many people.

Ken Ruettgers, *Packers tackle (1985–96)*:

We were sitting around talking one evening, me and my wife and Mike Arthur and his wife and Reggie and Keith Jackson. I had been baptized as an infant and had never made a public proclamation with my baptism. So we thought, Why not? The next night we went into the locker room, and Reggie baptized us in the whirlpool. It was a huge thing. It was the biggest baptistry I'd ever seen. Afterwards, we sang songs and prayed.

Joe Theismann, *Washington Redskins quarterback (1974–85)/ESPN NFL analyst:*

He was one of the dearest souls to ever put on a uniform. He was committed and outspoken in his beliefs, feared nothing, and his commitment to God was No. 1 in his life.

Mark Schlereth, *Washington Redskins-Denver Broncos guard (1989–2000)/ESPN NFL analyst:*

Reggie White was one of the greatest football players I've ever seen or lined up against. He was amazingly dominant and someone that a team spent a week preparing for. When an offensive line stepped onto the field, it was imperative to locate where White was to have some semblance of a chance at figuring out how he was going to disrupt your offense.

I'll never forget one of the first times I ever had to face White on the field. I was playing for the Redskins, and I didn't really expect to have to face him. At the time, the Eagles would switch him all over the line so that he'd occasionally face a guard. I'll never forget how I felt when I came out of the huddle and realized he was lining up to face me. I immediately started wondering what I'd done to deserve this butt whupping.

Off the field, there wasn't a hypocritical bone in his body. He affected many people with his personality, beliefs, and the stewardship of his life. He was one of the greatest and noblest men I've ever been around. Regardless of where you were in your walk in life, he was going to treat you with kindness, compassion, love, and respect.

***Eric Allen**, Philadelphia Eagles-New Orleans Saints-Oakland Raiders cornerback (1988–2001):*

You probably know we were teammates from 1988 to 1992. What you probably don't know is, he was probably the biggest influence on me from the time I stepped foot into Philadelphia until now, more so off the field than on. We continued to stay in touch throughout my seventeen years since being a rookie in Philadelphia, and I have a great amount of love for him and his family. So, like he would do, please say a prayer for him and his family.

***Paul Tagliabue**, NFL commissioner:*

Reggie White was a gentle warrior who will be remembered as

one of the greatest defensive players in NFL history. Equally as impressive as his achievements on the field was the positive impact he made off the field and the way he served as a positive influence on so many young people.

~

Bob Harlan, *Packers president (1989–):*

Everyone thought the last place he would sign was Green Bay. It was monumental because not only did he sign, but he recruited for Green Bay and got guys like Sean Jones to come here. He sent a message to the rest of the NFL that Green Bay was a great place to play. That's what changed the football fortunes of this franchise. It was huge. And everything got better in a hurry.

~

***Jeff Fisher**, Tennessee Titans head coach, who coached White for five years as an assistant to Buddy Ryan in Philadelphia:*

I've never seen a more dominant player. Nobody had the combination of strength, speed and quickness that Reggie did.

~

Michael Irvin, *Dallas Cowboys wide receiver (1988–99)/TV NFL analyst:*

He was a gift from God, and that's all you need to know about Reggie White.

~

Mike Ditka, *14-year NFL head coach with Chicago and New Orleans:*

As great as Reggie White was as a player, what I remember the most is that he was the best example of what being a pro athlete is all about. He was pure class, on and off the field. He was always tolerant of his opponent and never tried to hurt or embarrass anyone. I loved him as a player, and I loved him even more as a person.

~

Duce Staley*, Philadelphia Eagles-Pittsburgh Steelers running back (1997–):*

I remember when I was a rookie with the Eagles filling in for Ricky Watters and I was playing against Reggie. I gave him a cut block and then got in his face and said some things to him out of emotion. He came over to me and said, "Rookie, that was a good block, but remember what you are saying is to a child of God." That floored me, and I wasn't the same the rest of the game. He was a remarkable person along with being a remarkable player.

~

Tim Brown*, Los Angeles-Oakland Raiders/Tampa Bay Buccaneers wide receiver (1988–2004):*

[The] Bible says, "Don't mourn for those who are saints—weep for those left behind." Certainly, Reggie is in that better place. He was the first true, real football player to stand up and say "I love the Lord." That got my attention right away.

~

Gene Upshaw*, executive director, NFL Players Association:*

He meant as much to us off the field as on it. He had his name on the lawsuit, and he didn't get one penny. That's just the type of guy he was. His character, his integrity was everything any NFL player should aspire to be.

~

Steve Mariucci, *Detroit Lions head coach (2003–), former Green Bay quarterbacks coach (1992–95) and San Francisco 49ers head coach (1997–2002):*

One time we invited Reggie and his wife, Sara, to dinner. My boys . . . wanted to play football with Reggie. He was tired from practice, but he said, "Of course. Let's go." He told them to get their friends for a game in the yard. There must have been a dozen kids.

Reggie played quarterback for both teams, and I asked him to throw one to my youngest, Stephen. *Boom!* The pass hit Stephen in the nose. Stephen was really crying, mad. Reggie tried to console him and picked him up. *Whammo!* Stephen smacked him in the face with his elbow. Then he got down and ran into the house. Reggie spent the entire evening trying to get Stephen back on board. All night long Reggie tried to tickle him and giggle with him and make amends. Finally, after a couple hours, they were wrestling on the floor and having a good old time. Reggie was a big kid.

~

Robert Porcher, *Detroit Lions defensive end (1992–2003), on the day following White's death:*

This is such a loss. About two months ago, Reggie was in town on business and he stopped by the practice facility. We chatted, and then I went to get [Detroit defensive tackle] Shaun Rogers. Reggie showed him every aspect of his hump move, and when he was done, he gave Shaun his phone number and told him to call if he could ever help him. That's the kind of guy Reggie was—he could have kept all his knowledge to himself, but he wanted to share it with everyone and help make them better players.

Kabeer Gbaja-Biamila*, Green Bay Packers defensive end (2000–), who holds the club record for most consecutive seasons with double-digit sacks:*

He was a man who tried to follow God's will. He was a man after God's heart. He used his platform to share the Gospel. It was an honor to meet him, and to know he experienced some of the same struggles I do.

Ron Wolfley*, 10-year NFL running back, then with the Phoenix-Arizona Cardinals:*

One time after sacking our quarterback, Neil Lomax, White looked down at him and said, "Neil, Jesus loves you." Lomax replied, "I know. But what's your problem?"

Ron Wolf*, retired Packers general manager who helped land White as a free agent in 1993:*

I'll have to use that old Bum Phillips line: "I don't know if he was the best, but it won't take long to call the roll. . . ." I told him, "You're already a great football player. Come here and you'll be a legend," And a legend he is.

12

Reggie White Timeline

1961 — Born Reginald Howard White on Dec. 19, in Chattanooga, Tenn.

Late 1970s — Chosen All-America football player and all-state basketball player at Howard High School in Chattanooga. Named Chattanooga football and basketball player of the year in 1979. That same year named nation's top two-sport athlete; Patrick Ewing is first runner-up. Career goals are to become professional football player and minister.

1980 — Begins collegiate career at University of Tennessee in Knoxville as a defensive tackle. Registers two sacks and 51 tackles as a freshman.

1981 — Records eight sacks and 95 tackles as a sophomore.

1982 — Logs seven sacks and 47 tackles as a junior.

1983 — Stands 6–5 and weighs 290 pounds as a senior. Registers school-record fifteen sacks, including school-record four against The Citadel. Finishes with school-record 32 career sacks. Records 100 tackles, 72 of them solo. Draws little notice early, then bursts to prominence in sixth game of season. Named Southeastern Conference defensive player of the year. Is consensus All-SEC pick and unanimous All-America selection. Named Volunteers' team captain. Hula Bowl and Japan Bowl participant after senior season. Named MVP of the Japan Bowl.

1984 — Chosen as territorial draft pick of Memphis Showboats of United States Football League. Leads Showboats with 11 sacks. Named to USFL all-rookie team. NFL's Philadelphia Eagles make him their top pick, and fourth overall pick, in supplemental draft of USFL players.

1985 — Leads Showboats with 12.5 sacks. In 34 starts over two seasons, records 23.5 sacks, 192 tackles (120 unassisted), and forces seven fumbles. When USFL folds after spring season, joins NFL's Philadelphia Eagles in Week 4. Starts at left defensive end for next eight seasons. Registers 13 sacks during '85 season, sharing team lead with right defensive end Greg Brown. Named NFC defensive rookie of year. Marries Sara Copeland.

1986 — Leads Eagles with 18 sacks, splitting time between left and right defensive end. Makes first of 13 consecutive Pro Bowl appearances; ties Pro Bowl record with four sacks and is named game's most valuable player. Son Jeremy born on May 12.

1987 — Scores one and only NFL touchdown on 70-yard strip-and-return of quarterback Doug Williams in season-opening loss to Washington Redskins. Voted consensus NFL defensive player of the year. Named to Pro Bowl. Leads NFL with 21 sacks — an NFC record and one shy of NFL record — in just 12 games during strike-shortened season.

1988 — Leads NFL with 18 sacks, tying Mark Gastineau's NFL record for most seasons as league sack leader (2). (Kevin Greene and Michael Strahan have since tied the mark.) Named to Pro Bowl. Daughter Jecolia born on May 24.

1989 — Logs 11 sacks, second on Eagles behind right defensive end Clyde Simmons's 15.5 sacks. Named to Pro Bowl.

1990 — Leads Eagles with 14 sacks. Has first career interception on deflected pass by Washington's Jeff Rutledge and returns it 33 yards. Named to fifth straight Pro Bowl.

1991 — Leads Eagles with 15 sacks. Has three sacks, two forced fumbles, and tips a Don Majkowski pass to teammate Mike Golic, who intercepts, in season-opening 20–3 victory over Packers at Lambeau Field. Gets second career interception when Golic tips Boomer Esiason pass to him in game against Bengals. Named to Pro Bowl. Named to University of Tennessee's all-time team. Spends Friday afternoons on Philadelphia street corners, speaking to young people about drugs, alcohol, and education.

1992 — Records 14 sacks, second on Eagles behind Simmons's 19. Named to Pro Bowl. Given Byron "Whizzer" White Humanitarian Award by NFL Players Association. Continues speaking on Philadelphia street corners. In eight years with Philadelphia, finishes with more sacks (124) than games played (121), becoming the only player in NFL history to do so.

1993 — Surprises NFL by signing with Green Bay Packers as a free agent on April 6; gets four-year, $17 million contract. Teammate John Jurkovic gives up No. 92 to White, who wore that number throughout his career; Jurkovic wore No. 64 thereafter. Steers the team's defensive ranking from 23rd to 2nd in a single season. Leads Packers with 13 sacks. Sets NFL record of nine consecutive seasons with 10 or more sacks. Becomes NFL's career sack leader on Oct. 31 against Bears. Sacks John Elway on back-to-back plays in fourth quarter to preserve Packers' 30–27 win over Broncos on Oct. 10. Helps create Lambeau Leap against Raiders on Dec. 26, when he laterals fumble recovery to safety LeRoy Butler, who scores touchdown and jumps into stands to celebrate. Named to Pro Bowl.

1994 —Voted to NFL's 75th anniversary all-time team. Logs eight sacks, second on Packers to right defensive end Sean Jones's 10.5. Named to ninth consecutive Pro Bowl. Streak of 117 consecutive starts snapped on Thanksgiving Day because of injured elbow, but plays most of game anyway.

1995 — Leads Packers with 12 sacks. Named to Pro Bowl. Misses the only non-strike game of his NFL career, Dec. 10 vs. Tampa Bay, due to what is believed at the time to be a season-ending hamstring tear. Visits the house of head coach Mike Holmgren two weeks before Christmas to tell him injury has been healed by God. Creates Inner City Community Investment Corp. in Knoxville, Tenn., to provide small loans to small-business owners or entrepreneurs.

1996 — White's church in Knoxville burns to the ground on Jan. 8; Packers fans donate more than $250,000 to rebuild it, but it is never rebuilt and White distances himself from the church. Leads Packers with 8.5 sacks. Records only interception while with Packers, picking off pass by Seahawks' Rick Mirer and returning it 46 yards. Named to Pro Bowl. Packers have NFL's best defense, go 13–3, and advance to Super Bowl XXXI.

1997 — Establishes Super Bowl record with three sacks as Packers win Super Bowl XXXI, beating New England Patriots 35–21 on Jan. 26. Leads Packers with 11 sacks. Named to Pro Bowl. Creates Urban Hope in Green Bay for people starting their own businesses. Opens Reggie White's Pro Shop in Green Bay. Stars in *Reggie's Prayer*, an inspirational film about a football player who retires to work with at-risk teens. Loses to former NFL player Steve McMichael in a pay-per-view pro wrestling match. Appears with Olympic star Kerri Strug as a gymnastics coach on CBS's *Touched by an Angel.*

1998 — Makes controversial speech to Wisconsin state legislature in March, criticizing homosexuality and using ethnic stereotypes to describe the gifts of each race; he later apologizes. Announces plans for Reggie White Studios, a film production and distribution company; *Barnstormin'*, a film on the NFL's early days is to be its first release. Retires from football for one day before season, then says God told him he needed to play again and returns to Packers. Leads Packers with 16 sacks. Voted consensus NFL defensive player of the year for second time. Voted to Pro Bowl for record 13th consecutive season. Finishes career with Packers with team-record 68.5 sacks and is the only player in league history to have 10 or more sacks in nine consecutive seasons. Reaches 100 sacks in 93 games—21 games quicker than No. 2 Lawrence Taylor. Sacks 73 different quarterbacks. Ties for most postseason sacks all-time, with 12.

1999 — Submits letter of retirement to Packers on Feb. 15. Takes year off from football. Packers retire his No. 92 jersey—but not his number—on Oct. 10. An emotional White tells the crowd: "I have always been honored and privileged to have been a Packer, and I will always be a Packer." Gov. Tommy Thompson declares Oct. 10 Reggie White Day in Wisconsin. Still, White is reportedly miffed at being honored on the Sunday night game against Tampa Bay, rather than an upcoming Monday night game against Seattle and former coach Mike Holmgren.

2000 — Comes out of retirement for one last season with Carolina Panthers, then retires for good. Starts all 16 games but logs career-low 5.5 sacks and 27 tackles. Plays against Packers on Nov. 27, a 31–14 Carolina home victory. "I miss it there immensely," he says of Green Bay before game. Finishes career with 198 sacks, then an NFL record. (Washington's Bruce Smith breaks career record in 2003, with 200 sacks.)

2002 — Inducted into College Football Hall of Fame, the 18th University of Tennessee player or coach to be so honored.

2003 — Selected first honorary member of Vince Lombardi Titletown Legends, a charitable organization of former Packer players. Partners with Washington Redskins coach Joe Gibbs, also a NASCAR racing team owner, to fund minority drivers for several late-model teams.

2004 — Elected to Peach Bowl Hall of Fame, having recorded eight tackles (seven solo) and one tackle for loss in 1982 game against Iowa. Inducted into Tennessee Sports Hall of Fame in his first year of eligibility.

Dec. 26, 2004 — Dies at Presbyterian Hospital in Huntersville, N.C. He is 43. Cause of death isn't immediately known, but a family spokesman says White had a respiratory ailment for several years that affected his sleep.

Sept. 18, 2005 — Packers retire White's No. 92 during halftime ceremonies of home opener against Cleveland Browns.

Contributors: Jeff Ash, greenbaypressgazette.com; others.

Notes

Chapter Two

1. White, Reggie with Jim Denney. *Reggie White—In the Trenches: The Autobiography*. Nashville, Tenn.: Thomas Nelson Publishers, 1997, 40–41, 43.

Chapter Three

1. White, Reggie with Jim Denney. *Reggie White—In the Trenches: The Autobiography*. Nashville, Tenn.: Thomas Nelson Publishers, 1997, 56.
2. Ibid., 58.
3. Ross, Alan. *Big Orange Wisdom*. Nashville, Tenn.: Walnut Grove Press, 1999, 54.
4. Ibid.

Chapter Four

1. White, Reggie and Terry Hill. *Reggie White: Minister of Defense*. Brentwood, Tenn.: Wolgemuth & Hyatt, Publishers, Inc., 1991, 37.
2. White, Reggie with Jim Denney. *Reggie White—In the Trenches: The Autobiography*. Nashville, Tenn.: Thomas Nelson Publishers, 1997, 62.

Chapter Five

1. Howard, Ron and Michael Gilbert. *Philadelphia Eagles 1992 Media Guide*. Philadelphia: Packard Press, 1992, 126.
2. White, Reggie with Jim Denney. *Reggie White—In the Trenches: The Autobiography*. Nashville, Tenn.: Thomas Nelson Publishers, 1997, 82.
3. White, Reggie and Terry Hill. *Reggie White: Minister of Defense*. Brentwood, Tenn.: Wolgemuth & Hyatt, Publishers, Inc., 1991, 128.
4. Christl, Cliff. "The Gory Years: 1968–91." *Milwaukee Journal Sentinel*, Jan. 20, 1997.
5. White and Denney, 103–104.
6. Litsky, Frank. "Bears Roll Past Eagles as Fog Rolls In." *New York Times*, 1989 Jan. 1, S1.
7. Howard and Gilbert, 129.

Chapter Six

1. Favre, Brett with Chris Havel. *Favre: For the Record*. New York: Doubleday, 1997, 23.
2. Hession, Joseph with Kevin Lynch. *War Stories from the Field*. San Francisco: Foghorn Press, 1994, 104.
3. Dougherty, Pete. "Soft sell lured White to visit, join Packers." *PackersNews.com*. 2004 Dec. 27.
4. Hession and Lynch, 104.
5. Berghaus, Bob. "Bob Berghaus column: White was the greatest pass rusher in NFL's smallest city." *www.PackersNews.com*, 2004 Dec. 27.
6. Favre and Havel, 151.
7. White, Reggie with Jim Denney. *Reggie White—In the Trenches: The Autobiography*. Nashville, Tenn.: Thomas Nelson Publishers, 1997, 17–18.
8. McDonough, Will, Peter King, Paul Zimmerman, et al. *75 Seasons: The Complete Story of the National Football League 1920–1995*. Atlanta: Turner Publishing, Inc., and National Football League Properties, Inc., 1994, 159.
9. Favre and Havel, 182.

10. Ibid., 151.
11. ESPN.com. "Memories of No. 92." http://espn.go.com/classic/s/Whitememories.html, 2004 Dec. 27.
12. Favre and Havel, 151.
13. Havel, Chris. "Gilbert Brown: 'Reggie was everything to me.'" *PackersNews.com*, 2004 Dec. 27.
14. Ross, Alan. *Packer Pride*. Nashville, Tenn.: Cumberland House, 2004.
15. Favre and Havel, 151.
16. Ibid., 73.
17. Ibid., 182.
18. White and Denney, 2.

Chapter Seven

1. White, Reggie with Jim Denney. *Reggie White—In the Trenches: The Autobiography*. Nashville, Tenn.: Thomas Nelson Publishers, 1997, 39.
2. Ibid., 59.
3. Ibid., 124.
4. Lackey, Skip. "Fire Guts Multi-Racial Church." *Knoxville News-Sentinel*, 1996 Jan. 9.
5. White and Denney, 27-28.
6. Schmitt, Gavin C. "Reggie White and the Cocaine Trade." *Writings of Gavin C. Schmitt*. strivinglife.net, Jan. 5, 2005.
7. Ayo, Laura. "Former Inner City Church minister gets 10-year term Upton is sentenced on drug and gun charges." *Knoxville News-Sentinel*, March 28, 2000.
8. White and Denney, 15.
9. Ibid., 195.
10. Ibid., 195–196.
11. Nelesen, Andy. "White wasn't a stranger to controversy: Defensive end's views at times caused a stir." *greenbaypressgazette.com*. http://www.packersnews.com/archives/news/pack_19192279.shtml, 2004 Dec. 27.

12. Pritchard, Dr. Ray. "Guest Opinion: Three Cheers for Reggie White." *www.illinoisleader.com/opinion/opinionview.asp?c=21686*, 2004 Dec. 27.
13. Ziron, Dave. "An Off-the-Field Obituary: The Death of Reggie White." *CounterPunch*. www.counterpunch.org/zirin 12282004.html, 2004 Dec. 28.
14. Carter, C. Van. "In Memoriam: Reggie White." *Across the Country*. http://acrossdifficultcountry.blogspot.com/2004/12/in-memoriam-reggie-white.html, 2004 Dec. 26.
15. Neven, Tom. "Reggie White: Fighting the Good Fight." *Focus on the Family*. http://www.family.org/fofmag/pp/a0024026.cfm, 1999.

Chapter Eight

1. Favre, Brett with Chris Havel. *Favre: For the Record*. New York: Doubleday, 1997, 183.

Chapter Ten

1. Nelesen, Andy. "Urban Hope will continue to carry out White's vision: Program helps participants start a business." *www.packers-news.com/archives/news/pack_19192605.shtml*, 2004 Dec. 27.
2. Ibid.
3. Ibid.
4. Kallman, Dave. "White's racing vision lives on." *Milwaukee Journal Sentinel*. www.jsonline.com/sports/race/jan05/296201.asp, 2005 Jan. 25.
5. JoeGibbsRacing.com. http://www.joegibbsracing.com/current_season/jgr_lm_20/lm_20_prhist.php.

Bibliography and Sources

Ayo, Laura. "Former Inner City Church minister gets 10-year term. Upton is sentenced on drug and gun charges." *Knoxville News-Sentinel*, 2000 March 28.

Blumb, Jeff, ed. *Green Bay Packers 2003 Official Media Guide*. Green Bay, Wisc.: Green Bay Packers, Inc., 2003.

Christl, Cliff. "The Gory Years: 1968–91." *Milwaukee Journal Sentinel*, 1997 Jan. 20.

Favre, Brett with Chris Havel. *Favre: For the Record*. New York: Doubleday, 1997.

Hession, Joseph with Kevin Lynch. *War Stories from the Field*. San Francisco: Foghorn Press, 1994.

Howard, Ron and Michael Gilbert. *Philadelphia Eagles 1992 Media Guide*. Philadelphia: Packard Press, 1992.

Lackey, Skip. "Fire guts multi-racial church." *Knoxville News-Sentinel*, 1996 Jan. 9.

Litsky, Frank. "Bears Roll Past Eagles as Fog Rolls In." New York: *New York Times*, 1989 Jan. 1, S1.

McDonough, Will, Peter King, Paul Zimmerman, et al. *75 Seasons: The Complete Story of the National Football League 1920–1995*. Atlanta: Turner Publishing, Inc., and National Football League Properties, Inc., 1994.

Ross, Alan. *Big Orange Wisdom*. Nashville, Tenn.: Walnut Grove Press, 1999.

Ross, Alan. *Packer Pride: For the Love of Lambeau, Lombardi, and Cheeseheads*. Nashville, Tenn.: Cumberland House, 2004.

White, Reggie with Jim Denney. *Reggie White—In the Trenches: The Autobiography*. Nashville, Tenn.: Thomas Nelson Publishers, 1997.

White, Reggie and Terry Hill. *Reggie White: Minister of Defense*. Brentwood, Tenn.: Wolgemuth & Hyatt, Publishers, Inc., 1991.

INTERVIEWS:

Bowles, Henry. Personal interview, Feb. 22, 2005.

Burwell, Mark. Personal interview, March 11, 2005.

Clark, Calvin. Personal interview, March 7, 2005.

Dickerson, Chuck. Personal interview, March 4, 2005.

Dotson, Santana. Personal interview, April 6, 2005.

Fulmer, Phil. Personal interview, March 11, 2005.

Gault, Willie. Personal interview, Feb. 25, 2005.

Golic, Mike. Personal interview, May 3, 2005.

Haupt, Dale. Personal interview, April 1, 2005.

Jenkins, Lee. Personal interview, Feb. 23, 2005.

Jones, Sean. Personal interview, Feb. 16, 2005.

Kremer, Andrea. Sara White interview, ESPN *SportsCenter*, Feb. 13, 2005.

Majors, Johnny. Personal interview, Feb. 14, 2005.

Marmie, Larry. Personal interview, March 14, 2005.

McKenzie, Raleigh. Personal interview, Feb. 22, 2005.

Nickerson, Hardy. Personal interview, March 14, 2005.

Prater, Herman Sr. Personal interview, Feb. 23, 2005.

Pulliam, Robert. Personal interview, March 12, 2005.

Quick, Mike. Personal interview, March 15, 2005.

Rodgers, Pepper. Personal interview, March 10, 2005.

Simmons, Clyde. Personal interview, March 8, 2005.

Walter, Tony. Personal interview, Feb. 22, 2005.

WEBSITES:

Ash, Jeff. "Reggie White timeline." greenbaypressgazette.com. http://www.packersnews.com/archives/news/pack_19191683.shtml, 2004 Dec 27.

Carter, C. Van. "In Memoriam: Reggie White." *Across the Country*. http://acrossdifficultcountry.blogspot.com/2004/12/in-memoriam-reggie-white.html, 2004 Dec 26.

ESPN.com news services. "White dies Sunday morning." http://espn.go.com/classic/obit/s/2004/1226/1953400.html, 2004 Dec 26.

ESPN.com. "Memories of No. 92." http://espn.go.com/classic/s/Whitememories.html, 2004 Dec 27.

Havel, Chris. "Gilbert Brown: 'Reggie was everything to me.'" *PackersNews.com*. www.packersnews.com/archives/news/pack_19194044.shtml, 2004 Dec 27.

Havel, Chris. "Stars come out to lay Reggie to rest." *PackerNews.com*. http://www.packersnews.com/archives/news/pack_19247136.shtml.

JoeGibbsRacing.com. http://www.joegibbsracing.com/current_season/jgr_lm_20/lm_20_pr hist.php.

JSOnline.com. "Tributes to Reggie White," http://www.jsonline.com/packer/news/dec04/reggiewhite-forum.asp.

Kallman, Dave. "White's racing vision lives on." *Milwaukee Journal Sentinel*. www.jsonline.com/sports/race/jan05/296201.asp, 2005 Jan 25.

Nelesen, Andy. "White wasn't a stranger to controversy: Defensive end's views at times caused a stir." *greenbaypressgazette.com*. http://www.packersnews.com/archives/news/pack_19192279.shtml, 2004 Dec 27.

Neven, Tom. "Reggie White: Fighting the Good Fight." *Focus on the Family*. http://www.family.org/fofmag/pp/a0024026.cfm, 1999.

PackersNews.com. "Fans share favorite memories of White" http://www.packersnews.com/archives/news/pack_19197320.shtml.

PackersNews.com. "Football world remembers White." http://www.packersnews.com/archives/news/pack_19191643.shtml, 2004 Dec 27.

PackersNews.com. "Readers recall on-, off-the-field memories of White."

http://www.packersnews.com/archives/news/pack_19229508.shtml, 2004 Dec 30.

Pritchard, Dr. Ray. "Guest Opinion: Three Cheers for Reggie White." www.illinoisleader.com/opinion/opinionview.asp?c=21686, 2004 Dec 27.

Quinn, Maxwell A. "Larger Than Life: A remembrance of Reggie White."

http://www.thegoal.com/events/reggiewhite/largerthanlife.html.

Schmitt, Gavin C. "Reggie White and the Cocaine Trade." *Writings of Gavin C. Schmitt*. strivinglife.net, Jan. 5, 2005.

SI.com. "Tribute: Remembering Reggie." http://sportsillustrated.cnn.com/2005/players/01/04/tribute0110/, 2005 Jan 10.

SI.com. "White Dies at 43." http://sportsillustrated.cnn.com/2004/football/nfl/12/26/bc.fbp.lgns.reggiewhitedies.r/, 2004 Dec 26.

Vandermause, Mike. "1996 champions are star-crossed." *PackersNews.com*. www.packersnews.com/archives/news/pack_19193534.shtml, 2004 Dec 27.

Ziron, Dave. "An Off-the-Field Obituary: The Death of Reggie White." *CounterPunch*. www.counterpunch.org/zirin12282004.html, 2004 Dec 28.

INDEX

Printed in the USA
CPSIA information can be obtained
at www.ICGtesting.com
JSHW082159140824
68134JS00014B/327